KIND WORDS

Strategic advisory

'Ros's professionalism, detailed knowledge and collaborative way she works results in a premium service and product. Her deep understanding of communications and marketing is of huge benefit to any size business. Ros is a delight to do business with and comes highly recommended.'
Julie Reid – Chief Executive Officer, LGeX

'Ros takes the passion and vision you have for your business, draws out the ideas you didn't realise you had and articulates these perfectly into a document that is usable and relevant to your business to define your brand, vision, mission and values to your clients and staff.'
Cameron McKerchar – Managing Director, Tudor Insurance Australia

'I have worked with Ros on many occasions and continue to because I know the quality results she produces for my clients and for my business. Ros's work helps clients get clear on who they are, the needs of their target markets and how they wish to be positioned in the marketplace. Every chance we get, we recommend our clients see Ros first as we know it will be highly beneficial for the final client outcome.'
Ricky Verkaik – Director, Zain Digital

'Finding Ros Weadman was a breath of fresh air. She listens. She gets it...Everything just works. She is professional, dedicated and timely. And she really knows her craft. Basically, I can't recommend her more highly.'
Ray Keefe – Managing Director, Successful Endeavours

'Due to the marketing activities that I am doing I am getting more leads than I ever anticipated... I highly recommend Ros to anyone that is looking to take their business to the next level.'
Andrea Jenkins – Principal Adviser, Jenbury Financial

Mentoring and training

'Working with Ros was like a breath of fresh air into my business. The outcome was business changing. I reconnected deeply with my 'why' and I am now able to see my business from a new perspective with a vision of where I want it to go.'
Deb Pace – Director, Pacing Dynamics

'The sessions we did with Ros were invaluable. Ros has a brilliant ability to empower you to broaden your thinking, to push you to think two or three steps above the issue you think you have, to then see the higher-level solution. My colleague and I often reflect on our sessions with Ros and the way our thinking has evolved as a result.'
Emma Williams – Strategic communications professional

'Ros's passion is infectious. She turns traditional marketing on its head and provides all the tools for success based on her unique marketing code. With Ros's support, I was able to create an effective marketing plan that really works.'
Caroline Ward – Director, Ki Creative

'Ros provides an excellent class with materials useful for real life projects and a comfortable environment for creating and sharing knowledge.'
Rebecca Burns – Strategic communications professional

'Great content. Absolutely loved it. All relevant and usable. Ros was highly engaging and provided in-depth training in a concise, easy to follow manner.'
Cr Tracey Hargreaves, Mayor, City of Ballarat

'The information was contextualised for our council and provided great insights to manage expectations when interacting with the media. Thank you.'
Cr Jessica Mitchell – Deputy Mayor, Campaspe Shire Council

'Useful REAL tools to take into public speaking and message creation. Thank you!'
Cr Sarah Gilligan – Deputy Mayor, South Gippsland Shire Council

'I learnt how to articulate my expertise, my value and how I can help people. I have language to communicate what I offer through my work and the transformation I deliver.'
Mabble Munyimani – Cofounder, MM Complete Wellbeing

Speaking

'Ros has this incredible way of taking you on a journey, making you feel like you're the only one in the room. Her insights and latest research are woven into compelling presentations that challenge you to level up your thinking and reconnect with your purpose. She has a genuine, down-to-earth style that leaves audiences inspired and ready to act.'
Claire Polatidis – Strategic communications professional

'Ros is an outstanding speaker – always engaging, friendly and inspirational. Her level of expertise is unequalled yet she is able to make each audience member feel that she understands their issue, their challenge and their aspirations. I've gained many insights from Ros and always come away feeling better equipped and eager to go forward.'
Maryann McIntyre – Director, The Inwriting Group

'As Chairperson of Women Making It Work, I can always rely on Ros Weadman to deliver exceptional workshops and presentations that align seamlessly with our goals. Whether speaking on vision, marketing, branding or business communication, Ros consistently leaves participants energised, motivated and ready to take action. Her presentations are engaging, interactive and packed with practical takeaways. A true leader in her field, Ros communicates with wisdom, eloquence and clarity, always leaving a lasting impact.'
Khatija Halabi – Chairperson, Women Making It Work

TRANSFORMATIONAL
COMMUNICATION

TRANSFORMATIONAL COMMUNICATION

The leader's handbook for communicating with purpose, power and presence

ROS WEADMAN

Published by Roslyn M Weadman and Global Business Publishing, a Division of Marcomms Australia 2025

Editing by The InWriting Group
Cover design and illustration by Ideas Ministry
Typesetting by BookPOD

ISBN: 978-0-6454388-5-7 (pbk) Ebook ISBN: 978-0-6454388-6-4

A catalogue record for this book is available from the National Library of Australia

'Leaders with a big vision and a bold message can change the world.'

Ros Weadman

For purpose-driven leaders who use their voice and power of influence to uplift people and create positive change in the world.

(And yes, this book is also dedicated to the elimination of boring, mind-numbing and uninspiring leadership communication. The kind that makes audiences switch off, tune out or walk away. Let's raise the standard!)

Contents

PREFACE   1

PART 1:   THE COMMUNICATION BRIDGE

   1. Stormy seas, shifting sands   9
   2. How great communicators have shaped history   17
   3. 20 lessons in transformational communication   41

PART 2:   LEADERSHIP COMMUNICATION IN PERSPECTIVE

   1. The illusion of communication   53
   2. The language of leadership communication   61
   3. Understanding transformational communication   73

PART 3:   THE TRANSFORMATIONAL COMMUNICATOR METHOD™

   1. Blueprint for becoming a transformational communicator   85
   2. Step 1: Self   91
   3. Step 2: Stakeholders   129
   4. Step 3: Storytelling   149
   5. Step 4: Structure   169
   6. Step 5: Skills   193

PART 4:   TRANSFORMATIONAL COMMUNICATION IN ACTION

   1. Amplifying influence through thought leadership   215
   2. Owning the narrative in high-stakes media interactions   229
   3. Building trust and alignment with stakeholders   251
   4. Commanding the room with impactful speeches and presentations   261
   5. Engaging employees and driving transformational change   271

EPILOGUE   283

ENDNOTES   285

ABOUT THE AUTHOR   293

PREFACE

Leadership communication is high stakes.

Whether you're in business, government, media or a community organisation, the leaders who most effectively engage hearts and minds are those who shape public opinion, influence decision-making and inspire meaningful change through conviction to a big vision and a bold message.

Across more than four decades as a communication strategist and mentor to high-profile leaders in government, business and community and through studying some of the world's greatest communicators, I've discovered that transformational leadership communication is not accidental. It's intentional. It follows key principles and employs techniques that elevate a message beyond the ordinary. These are the differences that separate good communicators from great ones – those who truly move people.

Hairs standing on end

I've seen thousands of speeches, media interviews, townhall meetings, public presentations and chamber debates in my long career. But few have produced the kind of visceral audience response I witnessed at a citizenship ceremony in the early 2000s when a leader's words, voice and presence came together so powerfully that it moved people to tears of pride and sent shivers down their spines.

I've been similarly moved by other leaders' communication on the world stage, such as Democratic Senate Candidate Barack Obama's unifying 2004 Democratic Convention speech, New Zealand Prime Minister Jacinda Ardern's compassionate yet strong address following the 2019 Christchurch massacre and Queensland Premier Anna Bligh's rallying *'We are Queenslanders'* speech during the devastating floods of 2010–11. The common denominator? They each communicated with purpose, conviction and empathy.

By contrast, I've also witnessed the opposite – uninspiring, robotic or forgettable presentations that caused audiences to disengage entirely. I've seen people yawn, check their watches, laugh uncomfortably, even walk out. What I've come to know is this: a leader's message only comes to life through their belief, voice and presence. When those elements align, the impact can be extraordinary.

Standing at a precipice

We're living in a time of profound disruption and deep uncertainty. Political instability, workplace transformation, artificial intelligence and social division are reshaping the way we live, work and relate to each other. Amid this turbulence, what people are yearning for is *real leadership*. Not just goals, but vision. Not just words, but connection.

In a time marked by distrust and distraction, the most influential leaders will be the greatest communicators. The ones who unite people around a shared, desired future and who communicate with truth, boldness and conviction. Respected leaders who navigate the paradoxes and uncertainty with strength and bring us all along on the journey.

Our destiny is not fixed. It will be shaped by the quality of our leadership and by how leaders show up, step up and speak up. In this new era, we don't need yellow brick roads or fake oracles. We don't need more polished perfection or performative soundbites. We need leaders who speak human to human. With courage. With heart. With purpose.

Standing up for our future

The pace of world change means everything is in a constant state of transformation. Leadership communication must evolve too. It must become transformational in nature: adaptive, responsive and rooted in a deep sense of humanity.

At times, leadership communication is about exchanging information. Other times, it's about building relationships or mobilising action. Transformational communication does all of these and it lifts our gaze. It keeps us anchored to a bigger vision and to what truly matters.

It's not just about influencing thoughts and feelings; it's about doing so with ethics, character and good intent. In an era of low trust in institutions and leaders, nothing less will do. Nor should it.

A leader's greatest asset is their ability to clearly communicate their ideas, vision and value, and gain support from their stakeholders, communities and followers. Yet many leaders struggle to cut through the noise and speak in ways that resonate. I've seen it time and again:

- vision lost in translation under pressure
- important ideas buried in overexplaining
- messages falling flat in rooms where decisions are made.

And, leaders quietly doubting their ability to engage hearts and minds.

The truth is, we don't rise to the level of our experience; we rise to the level of our communication.

And in today's fast-moving, high-stakes environment, communication is not a soft skill. It's a power skill.

This reality fuels my mission: to empower leaders to communicate with purpose, power and presence so they can lead with greater influence and impact. Because when leaders have a big vision and a bold message, and communicate it with clarity and conviction, they engage hearts and minds around a legacy that moves humanity forward. In these uncertain times, that is exactly what the world needs.

Standing for something

This book is a key plank of my work in empowering leaders to become transformational communicators so they can build trust and connection, inspire action, and achieve their goals and priorities. It's a practical guide and an aspirational call to lead with voice and vision. It's also a declaration of belief: that transformational communication is not only possible; it is necessary for our times.

The book is structured in four parts:

- **Part 1: The communication bridge**

  Explores why, in today's turbulent world, transformational communication is essential.

- **Part 2: Leadership communication in perspective**

  Outlines what it takes to truly engage hearts and minds, and the attributes that define transformational communicators.

- **Part 3: The Transformational Communicator Method™**

  Introduces a five-step method to help leaders evolve their communication to meet the demands of the new era.

- **Part 4: Transformational communication in action**
  Offers practical tools and strategies for applying transformational communication in high-stakes situations.

Standing apart

The new era belongs to transformational communicators; those with a bold message, a compelling vision, and the ability to inspire others through how they speak, listen and lead.

I hope this book becomes a valuable companion in your journey to communicate with greater influence and impact; whether you're leading a team, a business, a community or a cause.

Every act of inspired positive change, no matter how small, helps create a better world. And that, in my view, is the true hallmark of great leadership communication.

Rise as the transformational communicator you were meant to be!

ROS WEADMAN

PART 1

THE COMMUNICATION BRIDGE

1

Stormy seas, shifting sands

'In the midst of chaos, there is also opportunity.'
Sun Tzu, ancient Chinese military strategist and philosopher

Communicating in turbulent times

We are living in an era where the only constant is upheaval. The world has become undeniably VUCA – volatile, uncertain, complex and ambiguous. From political instability and rapid technological advancements to cybercrime, social unrest and the seismic shift in how and where we work, leaders are navigating unstable and unpredictable conditions.

These aren't just surface-level disruptions. They're changing the fabric of our institutions, economies and communities and, critically, the way we connect and communicate. Trust is fragile. Attention is fleeting. False information travels faster than truth. In such an environment, leaders are no longer just stewards of operations or strategy, they are stewards of purpose, vision and meaning. And in the fog of uncertainty, communication becomes their most vital navigation tool.

Every message a leader shares, whether spoken or unspoken, verbal or non-verbal, ripples outward. It can calm or inflame, build trust or instil fear, mobilise action or paralyse progress. That's why today, leadership communication isn't a soft skill. It's a power skill.

In these times of disruption and uncertainty, people look to leaders not only for direction, but for reassurance, belonging and a sense of shared purpose. They want to feel seen, heard and safe, especially when the ground beneath them feels unstable. They want to believe that someone is not only steering the ship, but doing so with both head and heart.

This is where the most influential leaders rise, not simply by having the right answers, but by communicating with authenticity, clarity and conviction. They face complexity with courage and communicate in ways that bring people together, create alignment and spark forward momentum. They recognise that in a divided world, their words have the power to either unite or divide.

In turbulent times of past, such as world wars, pandemics and natural disasters, transformational communication has been more than just a tool; it's been a bridge. A bridge connecting people by fostering understanding; a bridge closing the gap between ambiguity and clarity or between fear and hope; and a bridge bringing people together across differences of opinion, culture or geography. In the current stormy seas and shifting sands of a world in flux, those leaders who embody transformational communication will, once again, be the leaders who'll lead us to safer shores.

The disconnection paradox

It's ironic that in today's 24/7 communications-technology-driven world where there's never been so much opportunity for connecting with one another, many people feel more disconnected than ever. People can be both uninformed yet information overloaded, silenced yet shouted at, isolated yet bombarded, crave authenticity yet can't tell what's real or fake.

The artificial intelligence (AI) revolution, still in relative infancy, is not only changing our ways of working, it's changing the way we communicate. Like all technology, AI is a tool with upsides and downsides, and these depend on how it's used. While AI increases our productivity exponentially, early research suggests there are also social costs.

Research reported in the Harvard Business Review[1] in 2024 looking at how working with AI affected employees' connection with one another found that using AI at work is making people lonelier and less healthy. Across four studies, the researchers found employees who use AI as a core part of their work reported that while they felt more efficient and capable of doing more work, they also felt lonelier, were more likely to resort to alcohol and to suffer from insomnia than employees who don't use AI.

While mental health and wellbeing is more prioritised in workplaces than it used to be, the human connection cost of AI needs to be monitored and mitigated. Humans are a social species; it's in our DNA to connect with others, to be part of the tribe and feel a sense of belonging. With research showing that connectedness and belonging at work enhance employee engagement, productivity and performance[2], leaders need to ensure organisations don't lose sight of the importance of fostering employee interactions and relationships through human-to-human communication.

Research, however, shows that employees aren't only feeling disconnected, they're also feeling disengaged. The 2025 Gallup State of the Global Workplace report[3] found that in 2024, the global percentage of engaged employees was 21% (down two points from the previous year) while 62% were not engaged and 17% were actively disengaged. (These figures were 23%, 65% and 12% respectively for the Australia and New Zealand region). The global manager engagement level also dropped from 30% to 27%. The concern of having a largely disengaged workforce is the negative flow-on impacts on workplace morale, productivity and retention and, of course, the ripple effect on the customer experience.

I believe that behind this mass disengagement and the great resignation post pandemic is a desire for deeper resonation and connection to purpose. While there are many actions leaders can take to reinvigorate workplaces and workplace culture, central to any initiative is communication. Salary, flexibility and professional development are important material components of the employee value proposition. However, it's the human drivers of social connection, shared purpose and aligned values that give staff a deep sense of belonging, meaning and fulfilment through their work. While material offerings satisfy individual desires in the short term, the human drivers galvanise collective hearts and minds in the longer term.

When it comes to AI, use it as a strategic tool to leverage your communication if you wish, but always show up as a real human. Your humanness will always be your communication edge, because...

- Only humans have a smile.
- Only humans have passion.
- Only humans have gestures.
- Only humans have empathy.
- Only humans have personality.

And that's why...

- Only humans can lead change.
- Only humans can manage a crisis.
- Only humans can motivate teams.
- Only humans can advocate for resources.
- Only humans can tell stories with emotion.
- Only humans can persuade people of a good idea.
- Only humans can shift an audience to think, feel and act.

In a world characterised by high levels of disconnection and disengagement, a leader's humanness is their leadership communication advantage.

Mis- and disinformation and other fakery

Unsurprisingly but alarmingly, the World Economic Forum's (WEF) Global Risks Report 2025[4] identified misinformation and disinformation as the top global risk, posing a threat to societal cohesion.

According to the Australian Electoral Commission[5] *'misinformation is false information that is spread due to ignorance, or by error or mistake with the intent to deceive'*. Disinformation, on the other hand, is *'knowingly false information designed to deliberately mislead and influence public opinion or obscure the truth for malicious or deceptive purposes'*.

Mis- and disinformation are now pervasive across different platforms. Not only are citizens being impacted by fake information, identity fraud and growing scams, but according to the WEF report[6], the proliferation of false or misleading content is also complicating the geopolitical environment. It's being used as a *'leading mechanism for foreign entities to affect voter intentions; it can sow doubt among the general public worldwide about what is happening in conflict zones; or it can be used to tarnish the image of products or services from another country'*. Some of the ways the perpetuators use this tactic are by creating social media accounts with fake photos and names, or by inflating the popularity of their cause by using automated bots to bolster popularity of a political message.

We don't just have 'fake' when it comes to inauthentic media content that's designed to mislead, we also have 'deepfake', an even more insidious type of media manipulation. Deepfake is a highly sophisticated method of fabrication that uses people's faces, bodies and voices. Just today I saw an alarming deepfake video circulating on social media – that of a fake newsreader declaring that a particular country had declared war on another.

With fake news part of everyday vernacular, I fear we're numbing ourselves and disengaging from important societal issues simply because we can't tell if what we're reading, viewing or listening to is real or fake. So, we just keep scrolling until we come across something simpler and purer, that doesn't hurt our brain to decipher if it's 'ridgy didge' (real) or not.

Low trust, high grievance environment

Trust is the ultimate currency of relationships, yet time and time again, we see politicians, business leaders, government organisations and media outlets diminish their credibility through their actions and inactions. For example, the Australian public has shown it loses faith and trust in leaders when they don't communicate, or worse, when they go 'missing in action'. In 2019, former Australian Prime Minister Scott Morrison was perceived by the public to have stayed holidaying 'too long' in Hawaii while New South Wales was in the midst of catastrophic bushfires.

It's incidents like this that propel trust in our leaders and institutions downward and grievance upward. The 2025 Edelman Trust Barometer[7], a longitudinal global survey of more than 30,000 respondents, measures trust in the four institutions of government, business, non-government and media. The findings paint a picture of wide and deep mistrust. In the four years from 2021 to 2025, the percentage of people who think leaders purposely mislead has gone up by around 12 percentage points.

With almost daily headlines of political party infighting, making policy on the run, corruption on government-funded projects and ego-fuelled, tit-for-tat social media taunts by some of the free world's most powerful leaders, it's not hard to understand why trust in government and in our leaders is on shaky ground.

The barometer also found grievance to be high. Edelman talks about a crisis of grievance with six in 10 people saying they are aggrieved (have a moderate or high sense of grievance) against government, business and the rich. For government and business, grievance is partly underpinned by a belief that they make peoples' lives harder and serve narrow interests.

Alongside these findings, the barometer found that 31% of Australian respondents support hostile activism as a legitimate tool to bring about change. These respondents supported at least one or more of the following actions: attacking people online, intentionally spreading disinformation, threatening or committing violence, or damaging public or private property. This sentiment increases to one in two for Australians aged 18-34. Furthermore, the barometer found the majority of people are pessimistic for the future, with less than one in five Australians believing that things will be better for the next generation.

This dark outlook has major implications for all our leaders – government, business, non-government, media and community. How they respond, including how they communicate, will either restore trust or further diminish it. Words and actions matter even more. So, how can leaders address the trust and grievance crisis? Trust is earned by being a source of truth through the prioritisation of open, two-way dialogue, accurate and transparent information, genuine engagement and ongoing open communication.

Issues don't go away if they're ignored; they usually get worse. Mistrust and grievance are largely fuelled by uncertainty and fear. So our leaders must address the low trust and high grievance problem proactively and directly by reducing uncertainty and fear where it exists through effective leadership communication.

As humans, we're programmed to eliminate uncertainty in our lives. Our brains strive for what psychologists call 'cognitive closure'; a motivation to seek answers to ambiguous situations. While leaders don't always know how things will pan out, they can give people a sense of stability by reassuring them with clear, empathetic and direct communication. This is essential if we want to restore trust in institutions and dissolve grievances.

2

How great communicators have shaped history

'The difference between mere management and true leadership is communication.'

Sir Winston Churchill, Prime Minister of Britain (1940-1945 and 1951-1955)

Communication is at the core of our humanity; it's not only the foundation of meaningful relationships, it's also critical to successful societal functioning and evolution. In times of adversity, communication has been the metaphorical bridge that has connected us as humans.

When you search on the internet for a list of names of the greatest communicators in history, invariably you'll find people who had a big vision and a bold message. From political leaders to social changemakers to media megastars, the world has been changed by people who, through their communication skills, have engaged hearts and minds around a desired future.

Some are charismatic, others are quiet, but they are all mighty in their strength of conviction to their mission and message.

What follows is a selection of influential leaders, some with leadership titles and others whose leadership is by virtue of their just cause.

These people have changed the course of history through their powerful communication style and techniques. And in so doing, they have united people through times of change, crisis and conflict.

Sir Winston Churchill

Sir Winston Churchill, twice British Prime Minister, from 1940-1945 and 1951-1955, is one of the greatest orators of all time. Testament to his genius was winning the Nobel Prize for Literature in 1953. The citation for the prize specifically noted his *'mastery of historical and biographical description as well as brilliant oratory in defending exalted human values'*[8].

Churchill's leadership style has been described as action-centred and bureaucratic by some, and charismatic and transformational by others. Few, however, would differ in their opinion of his communication style, which was courageous, optimistic, forthright and inspirational. He is particularly remembered for his powerful words, stoic optimism and oratory skill in uniting a nation during World War II. Through masterful communication, he was able to convey his message to millions who would gather around their radios to listen to his speeches. The news was fundamentally bad, as the odds were against the Allies, but he was still able to instil hope in adversity through his courage, conviction and candidness.

Churchill revealed his belief in the immense power of effective speaking, when he said:

> *'Of all the talents bestowed upon men, none is so precious as the gift of oratory. He who enjoys it wields a power more durable than that of a great king. He is an independent force in the world. Abandoned by his party, betrayed by his friends, stripped of his offices, whoever can command this power is still formidable.'*[9]

Churchill is known to have spent hours crafting his message so it would resonate deeply within the psyches of British people so they would rally with him against Hitler and the scourge of Nazism. The below excerpts from three of Churchill's speeches to the House of Commons in 1940 highlight his masterful wordsmithing ability.

The 'Blood, Toil, Tears and Sweat' speech:

> *'I beg to move, That this House welcomes the formation of a Government representing the united and inflexible resolve of the nation to prosecute the war with Germany to a victorious conclusion... We have before us an ordeal of the most grievous kind. We have before us many, many long months of struggle and of suffering. You ask, what is our policy? I can say: It is to wage war, by sea, land and air, with all our might and with all the strength that God can give us; to wage war against a monstrous tyranny, never surpassed in the dark, lamentable catalogue of human crime. That is our policy. You ask, what is our aim? I can answer in one word: It is victory, victory at all costs, victory in spite of all terror, victory, however long and hard the road may be; for without victory, there is no survival. Let that be realised; no survival for the British Empire, no survival for all that the British Empire has stood for, no survival for the urge and impulse of the ages, that mankind will move forward towards its goal. But I take up my task with buoyancy and hope. I feel sure that our cause will not be suffered to fail among men. At this time I feel entitled to claim the aid of all, and I say, "Come then, let us go forward together with our united strength".'*[10]

First speech as Prime Minister to the House of Commons, 13 May 1940

The 'We shall fight' speech:

> *'...Even though large tracts of Europe and many old and famous States have fallen or may fall into the grip of the Gestapo and all the odious apparatus of Nazi rule, we shall not flag or fail.*

We shall go on to the end, we shall fight in France, we shall fight on the seas and oceans, we shall fight with growing confidence and growing strength in the air, we shall defend our Island, whatever the cost may be, we shall fight on the beaches, we shall fight on the landing grounds, we shall fight in the fields and in the streets, we shall fight in the hills; we shall never surrender, and even if, which I do not for a moment believe, this Island or a large part of it were subjugated and starving, then our Empire beyond the seas, armed and guarded by the British Fleet, would carry on the struggle, until, in God's good time, the New World, with all its power and might, steps forth to the rescue and the liberation of the old.'[11]

Delivered in the House of Commons, 4 June 1940

The 'Finest Hour' speech:

'...Hitler knows that he will have to break us in this Island or lose the war. If we can stand up to him, all Europe may be free and the life of the world may move forward into broad, sunlit uplands. But if we fail, then the whole world, including the United States, including all that we have known and cared for, will sink into the abyss of a new Dark Age made more sinister, and perhaps more protracted, by the lights of perverted science.

Let us therefore brace ourselves to our duties, and so bear ourselves that if the British Empire and its Commonwealth last for a thousand years, men will still say, 'This was their finest hour.'[12]

Delivered in the House of Commons, 18 June 1940

Communication techniques of Sir Winston Churchill

- Relentless preparation; wordsmithing and rehearsal of every word.
- Inspiring rhetoric to appeal to both logical reasoning and emotions.
- Simple and compelling message – 'victory'.

- The use of emotive language, repetition, metaphor and powerful imagery painted a strong visual image of what the future would be like, in victory and in failure.

- Language patterns, such as the 'rule of three' and anaphora, repeating a word or expression at the beginning of successive phrases or sentences.

- Vocal variety, such as dramatic pauses for added effect.

Oprah Winfrey

Popularly known as simply 'Oprah', American TV host, producer, actor and philanthropist Oprah Winfrey, despite a very challenging childhood, became an industry icon and inspired millions of people across the world to pursue their dreams. Winfrey's life story is one of resilience, determination and transformation, and she has made it a priority to share her valuable lessons and inspire others to believe in their own potential. *'Turn your wounds into wisdom. You become what you believe….',* she proffers, suggesting that our self-beliefs and actions shape who we become.

While Winfrey doesn't have a leadership title, she is a leader of people through role modelling a way of being and navigating life's challenges with strength in vulnerability, compassion and self-respect.

Winfrey's communication style is warm, heartfelt, empathetic and authentic. She is a master communicator, who uses open, two-way dialogue and active listening to create a safe space to share. She earns trust and creates an intimate, deep connection with people.

Winfrey believes great communication recognises our shared humanity:

'… Great communication begins with connection. What makes us different from one another is so much less important than what makes us alike—we all long for acceptance and significance. When

we recognize those needs in ourselves, we can better understand them in others, and that's when we can set aside our judgments and just hear.'[13]

She also believes effective communication is two-way:

'Communication is like a dance. One person takes a step forward, the other takes one back. Even one misstep can land both on the floor in a tangle of confusion. That's the perfect moment to rise to your feet and get clear about the next move—to gently say to the other dancer, "What do you really want here?"'[13]

Communication techniques of Oprah Winfrey

- Storytelling, particularly use of personal anecdotes, to make her message more relatable.
- Embracing the power of vulnerability by sharing her own struggles and setbacks, allowing for growth and resilience.
- Listening to understand, embracing silence, without interruption or judgment.
- Open-ended questions to encourage people to share thoughts and feelings.
- Open gestures and open body language, giving the impression of nothing to hide.
- Inclusivity, interaction and involvement of the audience to deepen connection.
- Acknowledgement, celebration and reward to instil hope and inspiration.

Dr Martin Luther King Jr

American Baptist minister, civil rights activist and political philosopher Dr Martin Luther King Jnr (1929-1968) was a pivotal figure against racial segregation and discrimination in leading the American Civil

Rights Movement from the mid-1950s until his assassination in 1968. He is most remembered for his '*I have a dream*' speech, delivered to an estimated 250,000 people in Washington DC on 28 August 1963. America Rhetoric[14] ranks the speech number one in the top 100 American political speeches of the 20th Century.

Below is a powerful excerpt:

> *'...I have a dream that one day this nation will rise up and live out the true meaning of its creed: "We hold these truths to be self-evident, that all men are created equal."*
>
> *I have a dream that one day on the red hills of Georgia, the sons of former slaves and the sons of former slave owners will be able to sit down together at the table of brotherhood.*
>
> *I have a dream that one day even the state of Mississippi, a state sweltering with the heat of injustice, sweltering with the heat of oppression, will be transformed into an oasis of freedom and justice.*
>
> *I have a dream that my four little children will one day live in a nation where they will not be judged by the color of their skin but by the content of their character...'*

King's communication style was no doubt honed from years practising and delivering sermons as a Baptist minister.

Communication techniques of Dr Martin Luther King Jr

- Using language to create vivid imagery in the minds of the audience.
- Positive language and a clear message of hope and optimism.
- Use of repetition to emphasise key points.
- A rhythmical cadence that almost 'sang' the words.
- Speaking with deep conviction to his cause that conveyed a sense of urgency to act.

- Use of storytelling and parables to illustrate his points of morality.

Malala Yousafzai

Shot in the head by the Taliban while travelling on a school bus only made this young woman even more determined to stand up for the right of all children to education. Born in 1997 and raised in Swat Valley in Pakistan, Malala Yousafzai ignored the Taliban's 2009 decree that all girls' schools should be closed. She defied the ban and at the age of 11 became known worldwide for her blogs about girls' right to education. In 2012, the Taliban shot her in an assassination attempt. Incredibly, she survived.

Rather than backing down, Yousafzai's experience only elevated her voice to speak on behalf of the voiceless and to achieve her vision of girls' right to education, freedom from terror and female emancipation. Her courage, conviction and resilience can be heard clearly in her powerful words, spoken to the United Nations Youth Assembly in 2013:

'Pens are mightier than weapons.'

'The extremists are afraid of books and pens. The power of education frightens them.'

'I don't want revenge on the Taliban. I want education for sons and daughters of the Taliban.'

'One child, one teacher, one book and one pen can change the world.' [15]

In 2014, at just 17, she jointly won the Nobel Peace Prize, becoming the youngest ever Nobel Peace Laureate. The Nobel Committee recognised that despite her youth, she'd already spent years advocating for girls' rights to education, with incredible courage under extremely dangerous circumstances. Through her heroic efforts she had become a role model for young people and a leading spokesperson on the issue.

Some of Yousafzai's most powerful words were said in her Nobel Prize acceptance speech on 10 December 2014:

> *'...Dear sisters and brothers, dear fellow children, we must work . . . not wait. Not just the politicians and the world leaders, we all need to contribute.*
>
> *Me. You. We.*
>
> *It is our duty. Let us become the first generation that decides to be the last that sees empty classrooms, lost childhoods and wasted potentials.*
>
> *Let this be the last time that a girl or a boy spends their childhood in a factory.*
>
> *Let this be the last time that a girl is forced into early child marriage.*
>
> *Let this be the last time that a child loses life in war. Let this be the last time that we see a child out of school. Let this end with us.*
>
> *Let's begin this ending . . . together . . . today . . . right here, right now. Let's begin this ending now...'* [16]

Communication techniques of Malala Yousafzai

- Conviction to a big vision and a simple, bold message.
- Positive language, hope and optimism.
- Humility.
- Each word clearly enunciated.
- Vocal variety with changes in pace, volume and pause.
- Use of logical reasoning with evidence of the problem.
- Use of emotionally-compelling narratives.
- Anchored stance and strong eye contact with audiences.
- Repeated calls to action to resolve the problem.

Nelson Mandela

Nelson Mandela (1918-2013) transitioned from a tribal childhood, an anti-apartheid activist, lawyer and prisoner for 27 years to become South Africa's first black president, from 1994-1999. His lifelong mission was to end apartheid and the apartheid government for the purpose of South Africa becoming a democratic nation. Mandela's negotiations with South Africa's president FW de Klerk did ultimately bring an end to apartheid and ushered in a peaceful transition to majority rule.[17] Both Mandela and de Klerk were jointly awarded the Nobel Prize for Peace in 1993 for their work.

Mandela is described as a charismatic, transformational leader modelling a servant leadership style by prioritising the collective good over his own personal ambition, and characterised by stewardship, vision, compassion, forgiveness, resilience, inclusivity and humility: *'Do not judge me by my successes, judge me by how many times I fell down and got back up again'*, he said.[18]

In his 1964 trial for sabotage and conspiracy against the government, Mandela spoke from the dock at the opening of the defence case in the Pretoria Supreme Court, giving one of his most powerful speeches. His *'I am prepared to die' speech* epitomised his unwavering conviction to upholding the ideals of a democratic and free society. This excerpt is the final paragraph of the speech:

> *'...During my lifetime I have dedicated myself to this struggle of the African people. I have fought against white domination, and I have fought against black domination. I have cherished the ideal of a democratic and free society in which all persons live together in harmony and with equal opportunities. It is an ideal which I hope to live for and to achieve. But if needs be, it is an ideal for which I am prepared to die.'[19]*

Mandela gave another powerful speech at his inauguration as State President, Cape Town, where he said:

'...The task at hand on will not be easy. But you have mandated us to change South Africa from a country in which the majority lived with little hope, to one in which they can live and work with dignity, with a sense of self-esteem and confidence in the future. The cornerstone of building a better life of opportunity, freedom and prosperity is the Reconstruction and Development Programme.

This needs unity of purpose. It needs in action. It requires us all to work together to bring an end to division, an end to suspicion and build a nation united in our diversity...' [20]

Mandela's speeches were powerful declarations of his conviction to end apartheid and create a nation based on diversity, equality, democracy and freedom. He not only galvanised the hearts and minds of his nation, he earned international respect and support.

Communication techniques of Nelson Mandela

- Unwavering conviction to one big vision and one bold message.
- Use of contrast frame, with optimism and hope always counterpointed against the suffering caused by apartheid.
- Use of persuasive strategies [21], including logos, appealing to logic and rationality in relation to his claims of white supremacy, pathos, appealing to the emotions, such as grief and rage and ethos, presenting himself as a credible and trustworthy leader, with his background as a lawyer and leader of the African National Congress.
- Use of language patterns, including metaphors, repetition and alliteration.
- Grounded body, no swaying or rocking.
- Used pause to emphasise key points.

Michelle Obama

Michelle Obama, former First Lady of the United States of America from 2009 to 2017 and advocate for equality and empowerment, has become an admired communicator of her generation. With authenticity, warmth and a gift for storytelling, she inspires people to live with purpose, resilience and compassion. She blends personal vulnerability with moral clarity, offering not just commentary but a call to possibility.

At the Democratic National Convention on 25 July 2016, Michelle Obama delivered what has become one of her most iconic lines: *'When they go low, we go high'.*[22]

This phrase crystallised her philosophy on moral leadership. It was a reminder that when others resort to insults, fear or act like a bully (*'when they go low'*), true leaders don't stoop to that level. Rather, they maintain good character and integrity (*'we go high'*). More than a political statement, it was a motto to live by in everyday life.

Other inspiring quotations attributed to Obama include:

- *'Your story is what you have, what you will always have. It is something to own.'*
- *'There is no limit to what we, as women, can accomplish.'*
- *'Success isn't about how much money you make; it's about the difference you make in people's lives.'*
- *'Don't be afraid. Be focused. Be determined. Be hopeful. Be empowered.'*

Communication techniques of Michelle Obama

- Relatable storytelling by drawing on personal anecdotes about her upbringing, family and challenges to inspire connection.

- Moral framing by anchoring her messages in values of dignity, respect, service and hope.
- Direct eye contact, warm smile and grounded body conveying rapport, strength and confidence.
- Uses empowering language by inviting listeners to believe in their own agency and potential.
- Combines vulnerability with strength, building trust through authenticity.

Ronald Reagan

Ronald Reagan served as the 40th president of the United States from 1981 to 1989. Reagan's communication skills were honed over a long career in public domains, including starting out as a sports broadcaster, becoming a movie actor then *'a long side-career of public speaking as his acting career closed out. He traveled across the country meeting Lions Clubs, Rotary Clubs, Chambers of Commerce and any other civic-minded local groups'.*[23] However, it was as president that he earned the title of 'The Great Communicator', a title he humbly played down in his farewell speech after two terms at the White House:

> *'...And in all of that time I won a nickname, "The Great Communicator". But I never thought it was my style or the words I used that made a difference: It was the content. I wasn't a great communicator, but I communicated great things, and they didn't spring full bloom from my brow, they came from the heart of a great nation -- from our experience, our wisdom, and our belief in principles that have guided us for two centuries...'* [24]

Farewell address to the nation – 11 January 1989

As a charismatic leader, the use of emotional appeal was central to his communication style. As cited in a Regent University journal, a study conducted by Mio et al. (2005) of all U.S. presidents' inaugural speeches ranked Reagan as one of the top three charismatic American presidents in the twentieth century. This found '*Reagan appeared to a sense of understanding through this use of symbolism and metaphors that went well beyond the actual words*'.[25]

Communication techniques of Ronald Reagan

- Charismatic communication with high levels of expressiveness, self-confidence and emotional resonance delivered with passion and inspiration.
- Use of storytelling and metaphors to create a vivid picture in the minds of the audience.
- Use of humour and eliciting laughter to build trust and connection.
- Audience relatability by speaking directly to the people, such as in his farewell speech, '*All great change in America begins at the dinner table*'.[26]
- Drawing on his acting skills, effective use of body language, including facial expressions, posture and eye contact, to connect with audiences.

Jacinda Ardern

Jacinda Ardern, the Prime Minister of New Zealand from 2017 to 2023 was known for her inclusive, compassionate and empathetic leadership communication style, most notably, her handling of the COVID-19 epidemic and the Christchurch mosque shootings in 2019. I recall the most powerful image of her wearing a head covering and a pained facial expression as she respectfully and empathetically mourned those who lost their lives in the massacre, alongside their Muslim families.

Ardern's belief in a compassionate and open communication style of leadership, rejecting the premise that prime ministers must be aggressive and masculine, became a beacon of what effective and modern political leadership looks like. Ardern also championed an authentic political leadership style by speaking as not only a leader but also as a woman and a mother.

The below attributed quotes showcase her compassion in strength:

'From a personal perspective, I am so looking forward to my new role as a parent. But I am equally focused on my job and responsibilities as prime minister.'

'One of the criticisms I've faced over the years is that I'm not aggressive enough or assertive enough, or maybe somehow, because I'm empathetic, it means I'm weak. I totally rebel against that. I refuse to believe that you cannot be both compassionate and strong.'

'I really rebel against this idea that politics has to be a place full of ego and where you're constantly focused on scoring hits against each one another. Yes, we need a robust democracy, but you can be strong, and you can be kind.'[27]

Communication techniques of Jacinda Ardern

- Speaks with composure and compassion while remaining clear and concise.
- Authentic expression, such as speaking from her bedroom during the COVID-19 crisis.
- Open, transparent and inclusive language, such as 'we', 'our' and 'us'.
- Use of communication tools accessible to everyone, such as live Q&As on social media.
- Aligned verbal and non-verbal communication, with strong facial expressions and gestures.
- Spoke candidly about balancing motherhood and statesmanship.
- Use of pause, a slower pace and downward inflection to convey authority and certainty.

Barack Obama

Barack Obama was 44th president of the United States, in office from 2009 to 2017. He was a charismatic, transformational leader, renowned for his vision, inspirational motivation, steadfast resolve and profound empathy.

Obama was a purveyor of hope, not the passive kind but the proactive, action-oriented kind. This theme ran deep from his speech as an Illinois senator at the Democratic Convention in 2004 until his presential farewell speech in 2017. The below excerpts highlight his central theme of hope:

> '...In the end -- In the end -- In the end, that's what this election is about. Do we participate in a politics of cynicism or do we participate in a politics of hope...?

> '...Hope -- Hope in the face of difficulty. Hope in the face of uncertainty. The audacity of hope!...'

Delivered 27 July 2004 at the Democratic National Convention, Boston.

> '...And people took notice. And throughout, it was infused with a sense of hope. And as I said in 2024, it wasn't blind optimism that drove you to do all this work. It wasn't naïveté. It wasn't willful ignorance to all the challenges that America faces. It was hope in the face of difficulty, hope in the face of uncertainty. You proved the power of hope...'

Farewell remarks delivered 20 January 2017, Maryland.

Communication techniques of Barack Obama

- Positive language, with hope and optimism key enduring themes throughout his career.
- Inclusive language, to unite all Americans, no matter their background or position.
- Repetition with extensive use of the 'rule of three'.

- Rhythmic cadence of speech.
- Open and animated body gestures, eye contact of the entire audience, lots of smiling.

In an interview at Hamilton College on 3 April 2025, Obama attributed his speaking skills to five key factors:

1. **Practise** - *'I think that the first thing to know about speaking, writing, or communicating generally is if you practice like everything else, you can get better.'*

2. **Conviction** – *'I actually believe that the single most important thing about being an effective communicator is having conviction, believing what you say. At least for me, that's the most useful thing. If you know what you believe as a starting point, then you will naturally communicate that conviction to other people, and you will seem authentic.'*

3. **Writing it down** – *'Now, there's some mechanical things like actually write out what you're going to say.'*

4. **Tell stories** – *'Part of how to talk like a human is to tell stories.'*

5. **Be a good listener** – *'What actually made me into a better communicator was when I started actually listening to the stories of the people I was meeting.'*[28]

Brené Brown

Brené Brown is a research professor who, for more than two decades, has studied courage, vulnerability, shame and empathy. She's also a compelling storyteller, author of six #1 *New York Times* bestsellers and the host of two award-winning podcasts, *Unlocking Us* and *Dare to Lead*. She has given the world 'permission to be vulnerable'.

Through her research and teachings, Brown has inspired many to embrace new ways of thinking about leadership and human connection. She encourages leaders to be more vulnerable, authentic and empathetic in their communication. Through her popular 2010 Ted Talk *'The Power of Vulnerability'*, she has inspired a new way of thinking about vulnerability, not as a weakness but as a strength because *'facing vulnerability takes enormous courage'.*

Communication techniques of Brené Brown

- Uses storytelling to connect with audiences on a deeper level, making her message more relatable and impactful.
- Uses humour to build rapport with, and engage audiences.
- Uses personal anecdotes and stories with self-deprecating humour.
- Flips thinking on the definition of human topics, such as vulnerability and courage.

Volodymyr Zelenskyy

At the time of writing, Ukrainian president Volodymyr Zelenskyy had been leading a country at war for three and a half years. With a background as a former comedian, Zelenskyy was not a seasoned military person but since his country was invaded in February 2022, he has given the world a masterclass in leadership, characterised by courage, authenticity and resilience, and hope in the face of relentless bombardment.

He has also given a masterclass in leadership communication, rallying his countrymen and women around a shared purpose and gaining the support of world leaders.

> *'We are fighting for our future, our freedom, our land. Just as 80 years ago, during World War II.'* [29]

Delivered to a student community of major Canadian universities, 22 Jun 2022.

Zelenskyy uses strategic communication techniques, including shaping global narratives to influence public opinion, using video messaging to reach a broader audience, connecting people through shared values, and using historical events and experiences to evoke emotion and resonate with his audience. For instance, when speaking to a joint session of the United States Congress, Zelenskyy connected Ukraine's battle to the American struggle for independence.

Communication techniques of Volodymyr Zelenskyy

- Conviction to a simple message.
- Use of clear and straightforward language.
- High level of visibility and proactive communication.
- Calm and grounded delivery with open body language.
- Authentic and relatable, speaking his truth from the trenches.
- Adapts communication to diverse audiences to address their differing needs and preferences.
- Leverages technology, particularly social media, to disseminate information, stay ahead of disinformation and engage with a global audience.

Ruth Bader Ginsburg

Ruth Bader Ginsburg (1933-2020) was an American Professor of Law and second woman to be appointed as an Associate Justice of the Supreme Court of the United States, a position she held from 1993 until her death. During her tenure, she was a champion of human rights, most notably, women's rights. She used her communication skills and a strategic advocacy approach to advance gender equality and other social justice issues.

Ginsburg was renowned for her ability to persuade and influence through clear, logical reasoning and well-crafted arguments and evidence. Her calm and composed demeanour conveyed her messages with authority and impact.

Ginsburg was a stickler for clear and concise communication, particularly for the written word, and known for her ability to write in a way that was easily understood. In an interview with Professor Bryan Garner, published in *The Scribes Journal of Legal Writing*[30], when asked if she worked hard at her writing, Ginsburg said, *'Very hard. I go through innumerable drafts. I try hard, first of all, to write an opinion so that no one will have to read a sentence twice to get what it means'*. When asked about cultivating her writing skills, she credited her former teacher of European Literature at Cornell, and renowned poet and novelist Vladimir Nabokov: *'He taught me the importance of choosing the right word and presenting it in the right word order'*, which can make a big difference in conveying an idea or opinion.

Some of Ginsburg's most powerful attributed quotes include:

> *'Fight for the things that you care about. But do it in a way that will lead others to join you.'*

> *'Whatever you choose to do, leave tracks. That means don't do it just for yourself.'*

> *'Reacting in anger or annoyance will not advance one's ability to persuade.'*

> *'It is not women's liberation, it is women's and men's liberation.'*

> *'Real change, enduring change, happens one step at a time.'*

Communication techniques of Ruth Bader Ginsburg

- Clear, direct, concise language, particularly with the written word.
- Use of voice was slow with measured delivery of powerful words.

- Opinions and arguments backed up with well-supported evidence.
- Calm and composed demeanour.
- Used her presence and influence for strong advocacy.
- Communicating on social justice issues where she could advance causes through policy change.

Steve Jobs

A legendary business entrepreneur as co-founder and CEO of Apple and Pixar Animation Studios, Steve Jobs (1955-2011) was an extraordinary business storyteller. He is renowned for his ability to inspire a compelling vision for Apple, coupled with his charismatic and persuasive communication style, which significantly impacted the company's success and left a lasting legacy.

Jobs, however, didn't start out a confident or competent storyteller or presenter. But he worked hard on crafting his messages and delivery skills to ensure his communication was as impactful as possible.

He has many powerful speeches to his credit, including the 2007 launch of the first Apple iPhone which was a masterclass in brand communication. However, it was his 2005 speech to Stanford University graduates that stands out as his most inspiring and transformational.

Drawing from some of the most pivotal points in his life, Jobs urged graduates to pursue their dreams and see the opportunities in life's setbacks, including death itself. 'The video, viewed over 30 million times on YouTube, contained some of his most famous words, *'stay hungry, stay foolish'* and *'connect the dots looking back'*.[31]

Communication techniques of Steve Jobs

- Articulated a clear and compelling vision for Apple, inspiring employees and customers.
- A captivating and persuasive communication style that enabled him to connect with audiences on an emotional level.
- Used storytelling to make complex ideas simple, relatable and memorable.
- Deep passion and conviction to his cause and message.
- Used empathy – rather than focusing on technical details, he emphasised the impact of Apple products on peoples' lives.

Mother Teresa

The epitome of servant leadership, Mother Teresa (1910-1997), St Teresa of Calcutta, was a Roman Catholic Nun, founder of the Missionaries of Charity and winner of the Nobel Peace Prize in 1979. She devoted her entire life caring for, and improving the lives of, the sick and poor in India.

Mother Teresa's deep empathy, strong moral conviction and ability to connect with people on a personal level allowed her to effectively communicate her vision and inspire countless individuals to join her mission of serving the poor and marginalised.

Mother Teresa had a 'call within a call', a divine inspiration to serve the poorest of the poor. She not only inspired a movement based on love and compassion, she changed the world.

Some of her attributed quotes epitomise the enduring themes of love and compassion:

'Not all of us can do great things. But we can do small things with great love.'

'Spread love wherever you go. Let no-one ever come to you without leaving happier.'

'If you judge people, you have no time to love them.'

'Let us always meet each other with smile, for the smile is the beginning of love.'

'I have found the paradox, that if you love until it hurts, there can be no more hurt, only more love.' [32]

Her words often highlight the power of simple acts of compassion and the profound impact of love in even the smallest of actions.

Communication techniques of Mother Teresa

- Unwavering conviction to a simple message of love, hope and compassion.
- Embraced the power of silence.
- Rather than using formal communication techniques, her approach focused on active listening, observing and asking questions.
- Her actions spoke louder than words.
- Deep empathy, making all people feel valued and loved.

While the politics, religion and ethnicity of these influential leaders differs, what they have in common is their powerful way of communicating; their ability to engage hearts and minds in a way that is truly extraordinary, towards a desired shared future. In most of the above examples, the communication created a shift in people so profound it literally started a movement or helped end a war. This kind of communication has a name; 'transformational communication'.

Unlike like transactional communication, which seeks to inform, the purpose of transformational communication is to illuminate and inspire. Transformational communication, however, is more than just motivating people in the moment, it aims to influence, uplift and galvanise people for the longer term to achieve a shared vision or goal. To make the world a better place.

3

20 lessons in transformational communication

'Effective leadership begins with effective communication. If you can't clearly articulate the vision, no one will follow.'

John C Maxwell, leadership expert and author

Transformational communication can be used for good or bad. There are many global leaders in history who have used transformational communication techniques to manipulate, instil fear and for other narcissistic reasons. This book, however, focuses on those leaders who have used transformational communication in pursuit of a worthy cause, oftentimes to overcome some form of adversity.

Although those transformational communicators identified above have lived in different times and places, and had different leadership and communication styles, they share many principles and lessons in the way they crafted and delivered their message. What follows are 20 lessons I've aggregated from the transformational communicators I've studied as well as from my worked and lived experiences.

1. Vision

A clear and compelling vision connected to a just cause. They use words to paint a vivid picture of a defined outcome that solves a big problem and moves humanity forward. Examples are Dr Martin Luther King Jr's dream of equality of opportunity or Nelson Mandela's vision for a post-apartheid South Africa.

They also paint a vivid picture about what will happen if their vision doesn't come to fruition; what will happen by accepting the status quo. An example is Sir Winston Churchill's warning that anything other than victory in the war would mean the world would '*sink into the abyss of a new Dark Age*'.

2. Conviction

Every great message is backed with strong conviction. For it is passion, belief and unwavering commitment to the message that unites hearts and minds around it, and gives it fuel for the long haul. Jacinda Ardern's conviction to kind and strong leadership, Mother Teresa's conviction to love and hope, and Ruth Bader Ginsberg's conviction to gender equality are examples of how conviction to a leadership message is a powerful motivator for change.

3. Intention

A message delivered with intention helps communicate your desired outcome without ambiguity. Transformational communicators begin with the end in mind; they know, with clarity, the desired outcome they seek through their communication. While on occasions it might be just to inform or educate, most often it is to persuade and inspire; to encourage their audience to think, feel and do something as a result of hearing their message. Malala Yousafzai, for instance, was clear in her intention with defined and inclusive calls to action for leaders to end inequality of education for children.

4. Simplicity

Messages must be simple to be understood and remembered. Simplicity is characterised by clear and concise wording that gets straight to the heart of the matter, and containment of the message meaning within a single sentence. Malala Yousafzai's message of *'one child, one teacher, one book and one pen can change the world'* and Steve Jobs' message of *'Stay hungry, stay foolish'* are good examples of simple yet compelling messages.

5. Positioning

The bold messages of the great communicators have a distinct position. There are no shades of grey or sitting on the fence. Like marketing products and services, the aim is to position a message in the minds of an audience so indelibly, relative to other competing messages, that it becomes associated with the leader's name.

Message positioning is all about how a message is framed so as to convey a specific meaning. Sir Winston Churchill's message of *'without victory, there is no survival'* was framed strongly in purpose. It was also forthright and left no room for misunderstanding or confusion. Messages that lack a distinct position often fall flat because they fail to evoke emotion and communicate why something matters.

6. Relatability

Your message is important to you but it's only important to another person because of the meaning they give it. Messages are more meaningful to an audience when the bigger picture context is linked to our everyday lives. For instance, while Churchill was addressing his colleagues in the House of Commons, his messages were also meticulously crafted to appeal to the 'common person', knowing millions would be listening via the radio. Oprah Winfrey's messages were relatable through their inclusivity in highlighting that while we're all unique individuals, we're also similar to each other, '*What makes us different from one another is so much less important than what makes us alike—we all long for acceptance and significance*.'[33]

Jacinda Ardern's and Volodymyr Zelenskyy's use of social media gave them a relatable platform to speak directly to their audiences and extend the reach of their messages.

7. Optimism

The language of the great communicators overwhelmingly focuses on instilling hope for a brighter future rather than focusing too much on blame. They understand the importance of keeping up people's spirits in times of adversity, to be resilient, to be strong to get to the other side. There is always hope. Examples are Anna Bligh's speech during the 2011 floods where she said, '*We are Queenslanders; we're the people that they breed tough north of the border. We're the ones that they knock down and we get up again*'[34] and Oprah Winfrey's, '*Turn your wounds into wisdom. You become what you believe....*' call to action. While not playing down the significance of a situation, Sir Winston Churchill continued to reassure the British people by reminding them of who they were, and that together they would prevail and grow stronger.

8. Persuasion

For the great communicators to sway their audiences, they had to be persuasive. Their messages most often contained Aristotle's three rhetorical appeals of persuasion – ethos, logos and pathos – to build trust and connection with audiences. Ethos, an appeal to ethics, is established by demonstrating good character, credentials, and aligning words and actions. Logos, an appeal to logic, is established through logical reasoning, such using facts, statistics and evidence. Pathos, an appeal to emotion, is established through the use storytelling, such as sharing personal anecdotes and evoking feelings by tapping into hope. Nelson Mandela's speeches were masterclasses in persuasive communication, with the trilogy of ethos, logos and pathos abundantly clear.

9. Storytelling

Great transformational communicators tell stories and use metaphors to aid understanding and memorability, evoke feelings and bring their message to life. Storytelling is almost as old as humanity itself and is the primary way people build rapport, trust and understanding. Personal stories of deep lived or worked experience add weight to a message and human vulnerability connect an audience with a leader. Oprah Winfrey, Brené Brown and Michelle Obama use extensive personal anecdotes to deliver strong messages of life lessons learnt and to inspire empowerment in their audiences.

10. Call to action

While statements on their own can be powerful, a call to action within a message can make them even more resonant. The great communicators used both direct and indirect calls to action to empower, inspire and create positive change. Steve Jobs' message of '*Stay hungry, stay foolish*' was a direct call to action while Mother Teresa's message, '*Not all of us can do great things. But we can do small things with great love*' was an implicit call to action.

11. Active listening

Communication only happens when there's a two-way exchange, otherwise it's only information flow one-way. The great transformational communicators don't just trumpet their message, they listen to other perspectives and seek to gain mutual understanding through dialogue, if that's possible. Mother Teresa and Oprah Winfrey exemplify the power of active listening which helps people feel seen, heard and understood.

12. Vocal variety

It's not just what you say; it's also how you say it. Our voices are versatile instruments we can use to emphasise key points, convey meaning and have emotional impact. By altering voice volume, pitch and pace, and using pause strategically, we can engage audiences and have a bigger impact. Dr Martin Luther King Jr and Barack Obama, for example, both spoke in a rhythmical way, giving cadence to their speeches, while Sir Winston Churchill used dramatic pauses for effect.

13. Repetition

Generally speaking, messages need to be repeated several times for them to sink in. In marketing, they say it takes at up to seven exposures to a message before someone starts to take notice. The great communicators repeated their message often, not just for clarity but to ensure the message stayed top of mind. Dr Martin Luther King Jr, for example, repeated the '*I have a dream*' phrase eight times in his famous speech to bring vividness to his vision for an integrated and unified America while Barack Obama continually reinforced his message of hope. As Sir Winston Churchill is coined to have said, '*If you have an important point to make, don't try to be subtle or clever. Use a pile driver. Hit the point once. Then come back and hit it again. Then hit it a third time - a tremendous whack.*'[35]

14. Confidence

A message delivered with confidence helps a leader appear more credible, authoritative and trustworthy. Confidence comes through in many ways – the boldness of words, the directness of eye contact, and the use of voice and body with volition. The confidence of the great communicators is observed through strength of conviction to their message and passion to the vision they pursue. Confidence is also connected to the fact that many planned, prepared and rehearsed their messages and speeches many times before the actual public delivery.

15. Authenticity

Authenticity means bringing our whole selves to a conversation – our observations, beliefs, values and feelings – and communicating openly, honestly and directly. Jacinda Ardern spoke her unapologetic truth as both a leader and a mother. She also defended her values of compassionate leadership when she said, *'One of the criticisms I've faced over the years is that I'm not aggressive enough or assertive enough, or maybe somehow, because I'm empathetic, it means I'm weak. I totally rebel against that. I refuse to believe that you cannot be both compassionate and strong.'*[36]

Authenticity in communication style is a hallmark of the great communicators. Charisma, for example, the kind of positive, magnetic energy that draws an audience closer, was a characteristic of both Ronald Reagan and Barack Obama. On the other hand, the quiet strength and humility of Mother Teresa was just as impactful in conveying a strong message.

16. Open body language

Open body language, supported by direct eye contact, builds trust by conveying a sense of confidence in their message and letting people know they're approachable and have nothing to hide. Closed body language and looking away has the opposite effect. Volodymyr Zelenskyy and Barack Obama are renowned for their use of open gestures and open body language, which they use with volition to convey openness and emphasise important points.

17. Language patterns

Language patterns, such as the 'rule of three' and alliteration (phrases with words starting with the same letter) add variety to content, emphasise key points and aid memorability of message. The use of inclusive language, such as 'we' and 'us' is also a powerful language pattern used by great communicators to empower an audience, create a sense of shared understanding and belonging, and unite people towards action. Jacinda Ardern's use of inclusive language served to unite people, no matter their differences, every day and in times of crisis.

18. Alignment

Credibility is lost when things are out alignment. For instance, when words and body language are out of sync or when actions don't match words. Words, body language and actions must be consistently congruent for audiences to trust. The great communicators demonstrate consistent alignment between what they say and how they say it so there is no confusion about the meaning of their message. They also act in alignment with their words. Barack Obama and Steve Jobs, for example, were not only consistently aligned in their words and actions, they were also consistently aligned in their personal grooming, wearing the same kind of clothing each day.

19. Gravitas

People amplify their leadership presence and create feelings of respect and trust when they show genuine interest, exude a calm and confident demeanour, use direct, concrete and inclusive language, and use positive body language, such as standing square on, natural gestures and direct eye contact. Nelson Mandela, Volodymyr Zelenskyy, Ruth Bader Ginsberg and Malala Yousafzai, with their grounded presence, anchored posture and direct eye contact, exude gravitas and build a strong connection with their audience.

20. Preparation

Great transformational communicators know that every word and the way it's delivered can form a strong and lasting impression on an audience; so they spend time and effort wordsmithing scripts and practising their delivery. Churchill, for instance, is known to have *'drafted his speeches several times and wrote them out in a way that would help him deliver them effectively. He rehearsed passages, again and again, pacing his rooms, repeating them out loud, learning whole speeches by heart'.*[37] While many leaders have speech writers, Churchill is known to have written his own speeches until old age.

These lessons in transformational communication are more than tips and techniques; they're principles to abide by. And while transformational communication is often a hallmark of leaders who have achieved change on a large scale, it's a style of communication that can be embraced by leaders at any level who strive to get the best out of their people.

It is a communication style that, through its characteristics of clarity of vision, empathy, transparency and conviction to a bold message, aims to build trust, connection and collaboration to shape a desired future, together. It is, therefore, applicable to many leadership situations where motivating and inspiring people is needed.

The new era belongs to those leaders who unite people around a shared future and who, through their communication, unite not divide, engage not disengage and foster belonging not disconnection. This book is a red carpet for such a transformational communicator.

PART 2

LEADERSHIP COMMUNICATION IN PERSPECTIVE

1

The illusion of communication

*'The trouble with communication is
the illusion it has taken place.'*

George Bernard Shaw, playwright and critic

Basic communication process

Before we delve more deeply into leadership communication, we must first understand the communication process itself. On the surface, communication may seem like a basic process – you send a message to someone and they respond to it. Basic, right? Well, actually, no. The process of communication is quite complex, because there's so many factors at play.

The diagram on the following page shows a widely accepted model of communication.

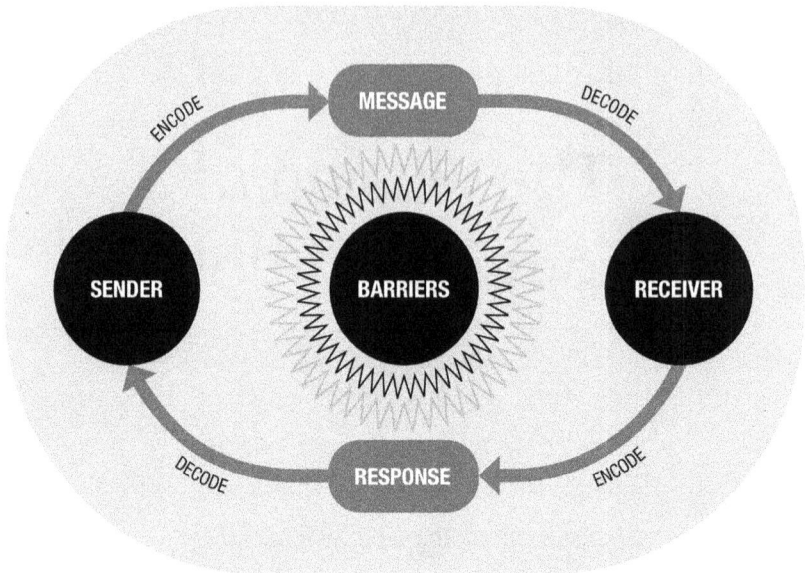

Basic model of communication

The process involves a sender encoding their message with a mix of words, sounds, symbols and body language with the intention of creating a shared meaning with the receiver. The receiver then decodes the message based on a range of factors, including their personal beliefs, values and perspectives, and their level of interest and concern in the topic.

The purpose of the communication can range from simple information sharing through to wanting to elicit a specific response, such as influencing the receiver to think, feel or do something. Based on the intention, the sender will encode the message to enhance its persuasive effect.

Messages can be conveyed to the receiver via one or multiple channels, such as via the spoken word, a letter, newsletter, video, telephone message, email and the like. Importantly, the channel needs to be a conduit that's accessible and preferable to the receiver.

Not all, however, is as it seems when it comes to communicating a message. George Bernard Shaw's witticism that, '*The single biggest problem with communication is the illusion it has taken place*' is accurate as there are many factors that can create barriers to a message and impact the effectiveness of communication.

Below are some of the factors that can impact the communication process and influence the receptivity of a message:

- **environmental** factors, such as competing messages, walls and background noise
- **human physical** barriers, such as a hearing impairment, hats and other headwear
- **psychological** filters, such as a person's existing knowledge, beliefs, values, biases and their level of interest in the topic
- **emotional** factors, including the emotional state of the person sending or the person receiving the message
- **cultural** factors, such as language and behavioural differences.

Other barriers that can impact the communication process include the content of the message, how it is worded, the timing and the relationship between the sender and receiver.

Being aware of barriers that can inhibit communication allows leaders to give more consideration to how their message may be heard by the recipient and not just how it is said.

How people process information

The way a person processes a message also influences the success of communication. People process information differently based on their individual values and beliefs, expectations, experiences and perspectives, and this influences both their understanding of the information and their receptivity to it.

The below diagram, based on the Neuro Linguistic Programming (NLP) communication model, shows how information received through our senses is processed and translated into our thoughts, feelings and behaviours.

Co-created by Richard Bandler and John Grinder in the 1970s, NLP is an approach to communication, personal development and psychotherapy that focuses on the connection between neurological processes, language and behavioral patterns. 'Nuero' refers to the brain and nervous system, and how meaning is attributed to experiences; 'linguistic' refers to language and the words we use; and 'programming' refers to our habitual and learned patterns, beliefs and strategies that influence our actions and behaviours. Understanding this elaborate information processing process helps us appreciate how our uniqueness influences they way we receive, interpret and respond to someone's message.

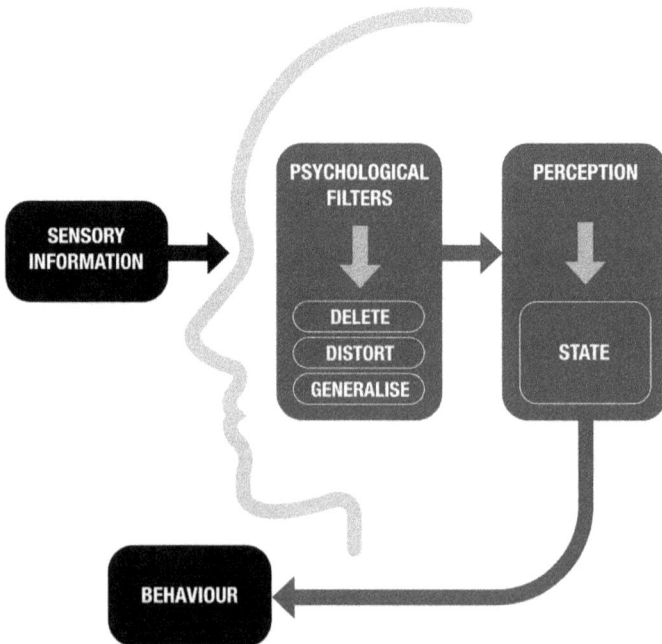

Basic Neuro Linguistic Programming model of communication

The NLP model of communication shows how we experience and perceive the world through our senses. While there are differing views about how much information is incoming through the senses, it could possibly be approximately 11 million bits of information incoming every second.[1] What is clear though, is we can only process a small amount of information at a time as it all gets filtered, possibly 50 bits per second, based on our values, beliefs, attitudes, memories, decisions, language.

Seeing is the dominant sense of our sensory system, taking in the vast majority of sensory information, possibly around:

- **Eyes** – 10 million bits per second
- **Skin** – 1 million bits per second
- **Ears** – 100,000 bits per second
- **Smell** – 100,000 bits per second
- **Taste** – 1,000 bits per second

According to NLP, filters cause us to delete, distort and generalise the information we receive. Deleting information means leaving some aspects out because they're not important or we just didn't notice them. Deletion is essential because of the overwhelming amount of information in our world.

Distorting information means we place more emphasis on some aspects of the information than on others. For instance, we can pay particular attention to a certain aspect of a person or an event.

Generalising information is about taking one aspect of information as being universal or stereotypical of a whole group. Generalisations can become our rules, or convenient assumptions, which means we may not pay attention to the exceptions, or outlying, less likely possibilities.

Together, the deletion, distortion and generalisation processing of information shapes our perception by creating an internal representation (pictures, sounds, words, feelings, taste, smell) of what it means to us. This meaning is highly individualised.

When combined with our physiology, this internal representation triggers a state of mind and emotional feelings that influence our behaviour, including what we say and do.

As an example, what do you think of ice-cream? Has this question triggered a mental picture, a taste, a smell or a feeling? This internal representation of ice-cream has influenced your mental state and behaviour.

The map is not the territory

Let's take the idea of peoples' differing internal representations of reality a bit deeper. In 1931, Polish-American philosopher Afred Korzybski coined the term, *'the map is not the territory'* to distinguish our beliefs from reality. The map-territory association is the relationship between an object and a representation of that object, the same as the relation between a geographical territory and a map of it. What I mean by this is that everyone lives in their unique reality. We don't see the world as it is, we see it as we are.

From a psychological perspective, the map refers to the internal representations, descriptions, assumptions or theories a person has about something. The territory refers to the actual, real-world thing, situation or phenomenon being represented in the person's mind. In other words, just as each person is unique, so too is each person's view (map) of the world. That's why the map is not the same as the territory.

Here are some examples to illustrate the concept:

- a person's description of food at a restaurant (their map) is how they experience it but it's not the actual food (the territory)

- a person's description of the weather (their map) is how they experience it but it's not the actual weather (the territory)
- a person's description of a piece of artwork (their map) is how they experience it but it's not the actual artwork (territory)
- a person's sketch of a house (their map) is a representation of it but it's not the house itself (territory).

It is important to understand that everyone has a unique perception of reality and this impacts communication. One person's understanding of a message (their map) may be quite different to someone else's understanding of the message, and both understandings could be quite different to the sender's intention for it to be understood.

This means that just because you communicated a message doesn't mean it's been received as intended. Words can mean different things to different people. Facial expressions, gestures and other body language can be interpreted in different ways. That's why leaders not only need to understand their audience intimately, they need to consider carefully how they craft and deliver their messages.

You're communicating even when you're not

Did you know you're communicating even when you're not? For instance, a person's or organisation's lack of communication speaks volumes. Every phone call not returned, every email not responded to, every update not given, every loop not closed, every piece of feedback withheld, still sends a message.

Those expecting a communication may ask themselves:

- *'Am I not a priority?'*
- *'Don't they care about me?'*
- *'Have I done something wrong?'*

Core values, such as 'respect', 'customer-focused' or 'collaboration', are proudly emblazoned on corporate posters and websites. Unfortunately, these core values don't always play out in reality when it comes to communication. While there is good intention, a leader's bad memory, lack of time or inadequate processes won't cut it for the person waiting for a response. Truth is, a void in communication breeds fear, judgement and disengagement. On the other hand, open and regular communication fosters understanding, trust and connection. And it's never too late to communicate!

Knowing the complexity of the communication process, the many barriers to communication and how we all process and interpret information differently, highlights three key points for leadership communication:

- We can't assume our message has been received as intended.
- It's up to the sender to craft their message for optimal resonance and receptivity (resonance, meaning to align the message with the beliefs and values of the audience, and receptivity, meaning to create conditions so the receiver is open to receiving the message).
- We need to remove any friction or barrier in the communication process, as far as practicable.

The language of leadership communication

'The art of communication is the language of leadership.'

James Humes, presidential speechwriter and author

A definition of leadership communication

Leadership communication is the approach taken by a leader to inform, guide and inspire individuals and teams towards achieving common goals, and the mission and vision of a project or organisation. It involves crafting and delivering messages, and communicating them in a way that considers the audience's needs, preferences and expectations. The aim is to foster understanding, earn trust and motivate people to act in pursuit of a desired outcome. Effective leadership communication isn't about simply sharing information; it's also relational in creating meaningful connections and promoting collaboration, and transformational in achieving positive change.

Of the top 10 critical skills for leaders identified in a global research report by Harvard Business Review, 'communicating for impact' was seen as the most critical skill leaders need to navigate the constant change and disruption of today's environment.[2] Respondents determined that without the ability to communicate with impact, the other critical leadership skills may not realise all their benefits.

Six common leadership communication fears and challenges

Even the most experienced leader can have fears and challenges about their communication, particularly when communicating to large groups and in high-stakes situations. The fears can manifest in debilitating personal impacts, such as anxiety, nausea and low confidence. They can also impact a leader's relationship with colleagues and followers, their ability to communicate the vision and expectations, and team morale and performance.

The following six fears and challenges rank among the most common I've come across in my work of mentoring and training leaders to be more effective communicators.

1. Fear of public speaking

They say people fear public speaking more than death. I dare say that's because we have to live with the consequences of our public speaking experiences. Jokes aside, this prevalent fear is not just experienced by people new to leadership roles; even seasoned leaders can fear public speaking.

A study by Kumar et al.[3] of 227 executives in a management education program found that low self-esteem was a significant predictor of higher anxiety around public speaking. The study also showed that boosting self-worth helps leaders manage anxiety in high-stakes speaking contexts.

The good news is, there are many techniques, such as box breathing, coaching to build self-worth and other approaches that can positively address this fear. Interestingly, however, many leaders say feeling some level of apprehension is a good thing as it shows they care and helps them perform better.

2. Fear of being judged

This fear is sometimes associated with low self-esteem or imposter syndrome, a fear of being exposed as a 'fraud' despite evidence of competence. It can cause a leader to withdraw and refrain from saying what needs to be said. For some leaders, a fear of being judged can be related to feeling self-conscious about their voice, body or body language.

Research published by the Center for Creative Leadership in 2025 revealed a top challenge for mid-level managers as 'personal limitations'.[4] This entailed overcoming imposter syndrome and *'projecting confidence while communicating effectively'*. The third top challenge was 'ineffective personal style' that can manifest as dominating interactions with others to lacking self-confidence to be assertive.

3. Fear of failure

Fear of failure is highly individual. For instance, it could mean suffering a 'brain freeze', forgetting their words, worrying that showing vulnerability will be taken as a sign of weakness or incompetence, or failing to have their message be accepted by the target audience.

Research[5] shows that leaders' underlying fears, especially fear of failure, loss of control or negative judgment, can have a negative impact on employee and organisational success. These fears can lead to decreased transparency and reduced trust in teams.

4. Fear of losing control

High-stakes communication situations, such as media interviews and large town hall meetings on a contentious public issue, can be daunting for a leader. This is especially the case for leaders who are prone to becoming emotionally reactive when under pressure. For instance, becoming frustrated, losing their temper or saying something they might regret later when faced with community outrage.

5. Fear of rejection

This fear is linked to the fear of being judged and is often related to a need to be liked by others. It can result in leaders shying away from communicating with large audiences. Leaders can also fear their message won't be accepted or resonate with their audience and, as a result, their authority as a leader will be weakened. They may fear rejection of their message will lead to a loss of trust and they could face resistance to their ideas and proposals in the future.

6. Fear of confrontation

Many leaders are concerned that their message will be challenged and they'll be forced to 'defend' their position if someone takes an alternative viewpoint. This fear can prevent them from addressing important issues or providing necessary feedback.

When leaders are self-aware and take action to address their communication fears, they not only build their confidence and competence in leadership communication, they also foster open, authentic dialogue with stakeholders, psychological safety, transparency and mutual respect. Learning to become a more courageous communicator is also essential for adapting to constant change and challenges, and ultimately achieving sustainable success.

What it means to engage hearts and minds

Origin of 'hearts and minds'

The term 'winning hearts and minds' has its foundations in military strategy. There are different perspectives on when and where the concept was first coined. For instance, French Army General Hubert Lyautey[6] is purported to have used the term during the Tonkin campaign in 1885. The term has also been linked with Britain's effort during the Malayan Emergency in the late 1940s and 1950s.[7] There is, however, agreement about its intent. And that is to gain the trust and support of local populations as part of the overall goal to succeed.

Engaging hearts and minds is a central concept and widely used vernacular in the field of professional communication, such as public relations and strategic communication. Professional communicators aim to craft a message that engages hearts and minds because it is a necessary precursor to achieving attitudinal or behavioural change.

Aristotle's formula

A central tenet of transformational communication is persuasion; convincing an audience of the worthiness of the vision, perspective or idea a leader is trying to communicate. Aristotle gave us the formula for persuasion two and a half millennia ago with his three rhetorical appeals – logos (logic), pathos (empathy) and ethos (ethics).

Together, these three rhetorical appeals provide the foundation for persuasive communication, particularly for the purpose of addressing public audiences or assemblies of people.[8] In the context of transformational communication, the purpose of using rhetorical appeals is to connect more deeply with target audiences to inspire people to think, feel and act towards positive change for a desired future. It is not to misinform or manipulate.

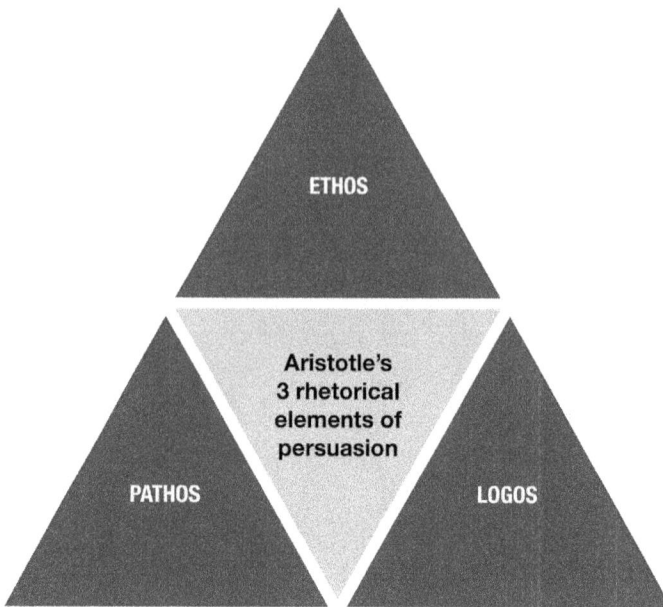

Aristotle's three rhetorical appeals of persuasion

Below is a brief explanation of each of the three rhetorical appeals.

Logos

Logos is an appeal to logic, to convince an audience of a perspective based on rationality and logical reasoning. Leaders can connect logically with audiences by using verifiable statistics, facts, research findings and other evidence to substantiate their claim, decision or action.

A leader's case should be clear and coherent, and able to be defended with counterarguments also grounded in logical reasoning. For instance, a leader may be proposing a new policy. They should first outline the problem, then detail their proposed policy solution, explaining how it addresses or solves the problem.

Logical appeals are best couched using concrete language, which is tangible, specific and 'real-world', such as 'cat' or 'tree'. It can also be things perceived through the senses, such as that which can be seen, heard, smelt, tasted or touched.

Pathos

Pathos is an appeal to emotions, to convince an audience of a perspective or to inspire action by evoking certain feelings, such as joy, curiosity or even fear, or tapping into their motivational drivers, such as the need for safety, belonging or significance. Leaders can connect emotionally with audiences by highlighting their values and beliefs, what they stand for and why it matters.

Leaders can make emotional appeals through storytelling, sharing personal experiences and giving examples through anecdotes and case studies. Emotional appeals are best couched in abstract language, which is more general and conceptual, such as the concepts of 'vision', 'values', 'love' or 'justice'. To make the concepts more real, a leader needs to use vivid imagery, by painting word pictures or by being specific with the details.

Ethos

Ethos is an appeal to ethics, to convince an audience of the character and credibility of the person making the argument or proposing the idea. Leaders can appeal to the ethics of an audience by highlighting why and how they are 'worthy' to speak to the topic. They could highlight their deep lived or worked experiences, credentials, accreditations, awards and testimonials. They could also reference their published articles and books to highlight depth of knowledge and expertise on the topic.

Leaders can also demonstrate ethos by being open, honest and transparent in the information they convey; by walking the talk and doing what they said they would do; by acknowledging their mistakes and working to correct them; and, by taking ownership and accountability for their words and actions without seeking to deflect blame to others.

For all three persuasive appeals, tone of voice and body language play a significant role in persuasive communication.

With great power comes great responsibility

Persuasion is part of everyday life. However, with what we know about the psychology of persuasion, and the power of verbal and non-verbal language, every leader and professional who uses persuasion in their work must ensure that their messages and actions are clear, honest and ethical, and not designed to exploit or manipulate others.

Seven reasons why leaders fail to engage hearts and minds

1. Focus on logic and not emotion

An important principle of communication is that your heart needs to feel for your head to believe. Effective interpersonal communication starts with the heart and follows with the head. Diving into the details (head) before establishing an emotional connection (heart) with someone can cause disengagement. Connecting on an emotional level before conveying factual information creates receptivity to your message.

The same applies in persuasive communication; the heart needs to feel for the head to believe. While logic provides a factual, objective and practical view of the world, emotions help us evaluate the data in terms of our values, inner wisdom and moral compass. So …

- when promoting your product, turn features into benefits

- when presenting your results, turn data spreadsheets into insights
- when pitching your big idea, turn salient facts into relatable stories
- when leading change, turn what and how into a compelling why
- when advocating for resources, turn the dollar contribution into a community outcome.

While we need to appeal to the head's logical reasoning, starting with the heart's emotional connection builds rapport, fosters trust and paves the way to open dialogue.

2. Lack of clarity

When a leader's message is vague or ambiguous, people become confused and fail to understand the intended meaning of the message. The flow-on effect can include misunderstood expectations, judgement and assumptions, distrust, disengagement and, therefore, poor outcomes.

3. Lack of confidence

As a leader, you may be confident in your leadership capability but lack confidence in your communication ability, particularly in high-stakes settings. Speaking with world experts and interviewing women leaders in politics, sports, the military and the arts for their book, *The Confidence Code*, Katty Kay and Claire Shipman concluded that, *'confidence is linked to doing'.*[9] So, if you want to be a more confident communicator, you need to act.

4. Inconsistent or misalignment of messaging

Alignment in words and body, and alignment of words and action is critical in leadership communication. When a leader communicates inconsistently or behaves in a way that contradicts their messaging, it undermines their authenticity and credibility. It also creates confusion, diminishes trust and damages their leadership brand.

5. Lack of transparency

When leaders don't communicate openly and honestly, such as leaving out important pieces of information or only conveying part of the truth, it creates suspicion, mistrust and disengagement. People are likely to speculate why the full truth is being withheld and jump to conclusions, such as thinking the leader is covering something up or doesn't think the audience is not worthy of knowing the truth.

6. Poor message delivery skills

Non-verbal cues like facial expressions, eye contact, gestures and posture all impact on how the audience takes in the message. For instance, no eye contact, folded arms, slumped shoulders and fidgeting hands can give the impression that the person has something to hide, is being defensive or lacks interest. On the other hand, direct eye contact, open body language, upright but relaxed posture convey warmth, openness and presence.

7. Lack of relatability

People respond to what they care about and ignore everything else. That's the reality of our information-overloaded world. To rise above the white noise, leaders can make a message relevant and relatable by connecting the bigger picture context to everyday lives, and by linking their idea to a pre-existing value or belief of the target audience.

While individuals have their own beliefs and values, research suggests that people like to be in sync with their peers. Dr Robert Cialdini's law of social proof,[10] for instance, shows that people will do what they see others doing because it makes them feel validated and safe. This suggests that communication messages are likely to be more persuasive if they convey that similar others are already behaving in the desired way. For those wishing to influence attitudes or behaviour, message framing can make your message more relatable and, therefore, more acceptable to an audience.

3

Understanding transformational communication

'Transformational Communication is a leadership communication philosophy that integrates transformational leadership practices with the timeless principles of persuasive communication. It engages hearts, stirs minds and mobilises action through purpose-led, values-based communication grounded in intellectual rigour and emotional resonance. This is the shift that turns communication into a catalytic force for belief, alignment and collective action.'

Ros Weadman, Creator of The Transformational Communicator Method™

Foundations of transformational communication

Transformational communication has its roots in transformational leadership theory; a dynamic and powerful style of leadership that uses communication to inspire people towards the achievement of a shared goal and overall success.

In *'The Transformational Leadership Report'*, American educator, author and businessman Steven Covey describes the purpose-driven and values-based foundation of this leadership style:

'The goal of transformational leadership is to "transform" people and organizations in a literal sense – to change them in mind and heart; enlarge vision, insight, and understanding; clarify purposes; make behavior congruent with beliefs, principles, or values; and bring about changes that are permanent, self-perpetuating, and momentum building.'[11]

The term 'transformational leadership' was coined by J.V. Downton in 1973 and introduced as a concept by James MacGregor Burns in 1978 in his descriptive research on political leaders. In his book *'Leadership'*[12], Burns says transformational leadership is about values, purpose and meaning:

'Essentially the leader's task is consciousness-raising on a wide plane. ...The leader's fundamental act is to induce people to be aware or conscious of what they feel -- to feel their true needs so strongly, to define their values so meaningfully, that they can be moved to purposeful action.'

The *Transformational Leadership Report* goes on to say that *'Burns became famous among alternative leadership scholars because his model of transformational leadership included an ethical/moral dimension that, prior to 1978, had not been infused into any leadership theory'.*[13]

Four key dimensions of transformational leadership

Transformational leadership has four key dimensions, often referred to as the 'Four Is'.

1. Idealised influence

This relates to the degree that leaders act in admirable ways that cause followers to want to identify with them. Transformational leaders exert influence by leading by example, expressing their convictions and what they stand for, role modelling high standards of behaviour and ethical conduct, and acting in alignment with their values and beliefs.

2. Inspirational motivation

This relates to the degree that a leader articulates a compelling vision that appeals, and is inspiring, to followers. Transformational leaders articulate a cohesive vision and inspire people towards this vision by speaking optimistically, painting a vivid picture, and giving a strong sense of purpose and meaning to the goals.

From an organisational perspective, transformational leaders connect the work of employees towards the achievement of the organisation's mission and vision. Employees are motivated because they understand why their work matters through connecting to a higher purpose. This has a positive flow-on impact on staff morale and retention as described in a Forbes article: *'Studies show that employees who feel their work has meaning and purpose are more engaged, committed to quality and likely to stay with an organization long-term'.* [14]

A 2016 global survey of 474 executives by Harvard Business Review[15] found that companies that align their brand to a higher purpose experience more success and connect more deeply with stakeholders. Key findings reported were:

1. 89% of executives surveyed agreed that a strong sense of purpose drives employee satisfaction.
2. 84% said it enhances an organisation's ability to transform.
3. 80% said it increases customer loyalty.

However, only 46% of the executives stated their company has a well-articulated sense of purpose guiding decisions and motivation efforts. Organisations with deeply embedded purpose were significantly more effective in innovation and transformation.

3. Intellectual stimulation

This relates to the degree to which a leader challenges assumptions, encourages active questioning and welcomes new perspectives. Transformational leaders encourage critical thinking, questioning of the status quo, and creativity in problem-solving to achieve goals and address challenges in pursuit of the bigger picture vision. This can lead to new, innovative solutions and improved organisational performance.

4. Individualised consideration

This relates to the degree to which a leader attends to the needs of individuals. Transformational leaders consider the needs of others by being empathetic listeners, making people feel valued and addressing the needs of individuals through guidance, mentoring and building others' strengths and skills. This approach improves an individual's self-esteem and inspires greater performance.

Applying the four dimensions to transformational communication

Applying a transformational communication approach to your leadership style involves embracing and embodying the four key dimensions of transformational leadership. The below model shows the four dimensions of transformational leadership overlaid with Aristotle's three rhetorical appeals of persuasion: ethos, pathos and logos.

I've added a fourth rhetorical appeal – telos – another term used by Aristotle that referred to the purpose or final cause of a thing. In other words, the ultimate end or goal of an action or entity. To this end, I contend that adding end purpose (telos) to ethics (ethos), logic (logos) and emotion (pathos) makes a message even more persuasive.

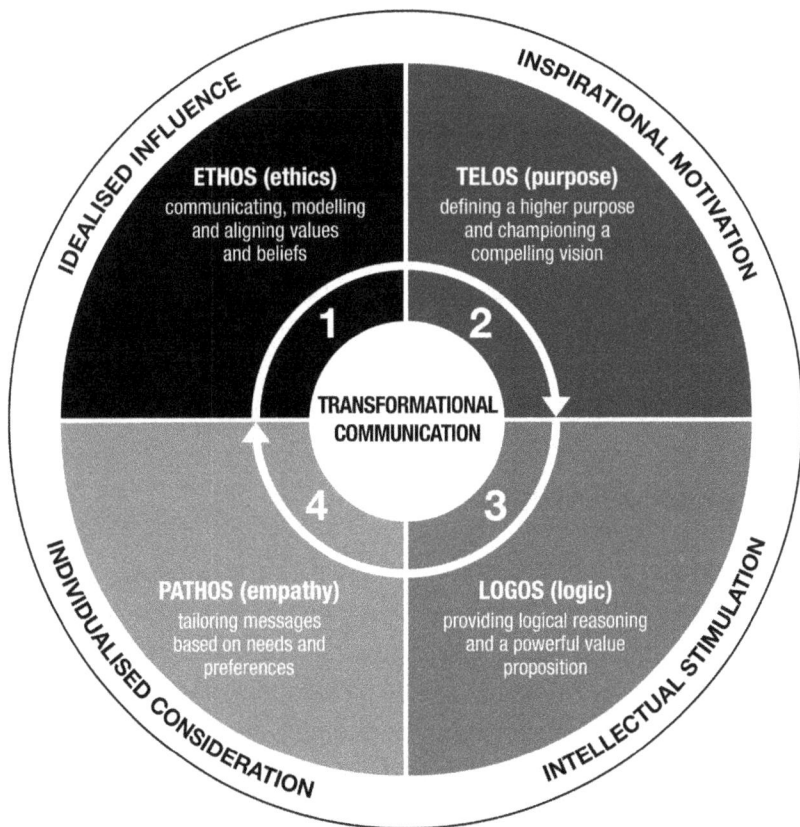

©Ros Weadman
Transformational Communication Model

Whether preparing for a media interview, strategy session, stakeholder meeting, Chamber debate, staff change briefing or other high-stakes setting, consider your communication through the lens of the four transformational communication dimensions, as follows:

1. Idealised influence

Idealised influence is about conveying character, credibility and ethics (ethos). You can do this by communicating, modelling and acting in alignment with your convictions, values and beliefs. This earns trust and respect and inspires your stakeholders, communities and followers to support you.

2. Inspirational motivation

Inspirational motivation is about shifting an audience's thoughts and feelings so they feel compelled to take action towards the achievement of a higher moral goal or end purpose (telos). You can do this by defining your higher purpose or worthy cause – your 'why' – and communicating a clear and compelling vision about what the world will be like when they deliver on their purpose.

3. Intellectual stimulation

Intellectual stimulation is about providing data and evidence that satisfy logical reasoning (logos). You can do this by backing up your decisions and actions with grounded facts and figures, defining strategic solutions and value propositions, and creating an environment of open communication where new ideas and perspectives are welcomed and shared.

4. Individualised consideration

Individualised consideration is about caring for individuals or groups of people so they feel supported and a strong sense of belonging and shared purpose (pathos). You can do this by being truly audience-focused, tailoring your messages based on needs, preferences and expectations. It's about being empathetic, using storytelling to engage hearts and minds, and providing support where it is needed.

In bringing it all together:

- When you convey **ethos** (ethics) you signal **character** and **credibility**.
- When you convey **telos** (purpose end / goal) you signal a worthy **cause**.

- When you convey **logos** (logic) you signal **cogence**, coherent and convincing logical reasoning.
- When you convey **pathos** (empathy) you signal warmth and **connection**.

In the context of a world in constant, fast-paced change and turbulence, leaders and their organisations, are always evolving, pivoting and adapting to survive and thrive. By adopting a transformational communication approach, leaders can rise to the challenges and achieve extraordinary outcomes with the support of their stakeholders, communities and followers.

A Forbes article[16] highlighting how transformational communication connects and inspires workforces, states that studies have shown that leaders who communicate a clear vision, appeal to values and emotions, challenge assumptions and coach employees individually, are better able to inspire discretionary effort from their followers. Furthermore, with the rapid pace of change and challenges, transformational communication 'will become even more vital for organisational resilience and success'.

Transformational communication in perspective

Effective leadership communication is situational; sometimes it's about having conversations for information exchange, sometimes it's about having conversations to build relationships; and sometimes it's about having conversations to drive action. However, in the current disruptive context, leadership communication most often requires an approach of the transformational kind. A communication approach that is responsive and adaptive to the new normal of workplaces, communities and nations being in a permanent state of transformation.

The **Leadership Communication Impact Spectrum™** shows the attributes, impacts and examples of three interlinked leadership communication approaches – transactional, relational and transformational.

Leadership Communication Impact Spectrum™			
Attributes	**Transactional Communication**	**Relational Communication**	**Transformational Communication**
Purpose	Achieve short-term goals and efficiency	Build trust, connection and mutual understanding	Inspire action towards long-term positive change and growth
Focus	Goal and task focused Information exchange	Build relationships through conversations of mutual interest and benefit Active listening	Inspirational motivation - inspiring action to move humanity forward Intellectual stimulation – questioning the status quo, exploring solutions Individualised consideration – connection on a personal level, uplifting storytelling Idealised influence – demonstrating principled and leadership of high integrity
Communication style	Language is direct, concrete, logical and instructive with the aim of getting things done quickly and efficiently	Language is open, direct, empathic	Language is more abstract, but also relational, inspirational and visionary

Leadership Communication Impact Spectrum™			
Attributes	**Transactional Communication**	**Relational Communication**	**Transformational Communication**
Motivation	Reward for short-term successes	Gain support and advocacy for mutual benefit and in pursuit of a shared outcomes	Shared values and beliefs, and a desired future
Audience impact	Informed	Interested and engaged	Motivated and inspired
Examples	Short-term goals Short-term task assignments Surveys and Q&A sessions Basic business transactions Formal communications News updates Instructive calls to action in emergencies	Informal conversations Networking activities Fireside chats Informal gatherings Awards and celebratory events	Long-term goals Inspirational keynotes Team building activities Community engagement conversations Visioning workshops Advocacy discussions Transformational coaching Project management

While each leadership communication approach has its place in various situations, the transformational communicator embraces all approaches as needed while never losing sight of the bigger vision and inspiring followers to come along on the journey.

Becoming a transformational communicator

The most influential leaders of the future will be the greatest communicators. That's why more than ever, the quality of leadership communication matters and so does your leadership message. We need leaders who give us something to believe in, who can unite us all around a compelling future, navigate the stormy seas and shifting sands, the paradoxes, the distractions, the fakery, the lack of trust, the high grievance and, bring us all along on the journey to our desired future, together.

The good news is, if you want to become a transformational communicator, you can because communication is a skill that can be learnt. A Forbes article by communication expert Carmine Gallo[17] states that according to Pulitzer prize-winning biographer and historian, and New York Times best-selling author Doris Kearns Goodwin, many of America's most influential presidents worked hard at developing their persuasive skills. Indeed, Winston Churchill worked hard to overcome a speech impediment.

What I've come to know after working with hundreds of leaders is that those leaders who truly know how to move a room have done the work. The work to build their leadership communication skills – to craft a powerful message, to tell a compelling story and to deliver a presentation with aligned voice and body.

We don't all have to aspire to be as influential or impactful a leader as Churchill, King or Ardern but we can develop the knowledge and skills to use our words, voice and body with volition to deliver messages that resonate so deeply that they cause a shift in an audience:

- A shift to *think*– to consider a new perspective, belief or approach
- A shift to *feel* – to evoke emotions like pride, joy or excitement
- A shift to *act* – to make a decision, form a habit or take a stand

But it takes time, effort and practise. In part 3 and part 4 of the book, I'll show you how.

PART 3

THE
TRANSFORMATIONAL
COMMUNICATOR
METHOD™

Blueprint for becoming a transformational communicator

'When leaders communicate clearly, they create alignment. When they communicate authentically, they create trust.'

Brené Brown, research professor and author

Transformational communication is not just an approach to connecting with people, it is a way of being and leading for influence and impact. Transformational communicators are committed to the highest standards of communication – operating at the intersection of purpose, principles and performance, bringing clarity to complexity and aligning thoughts, words and actions. Transformational communicators offer substance over sizzle. Their communication style is underscored by strong conviction to vision, calm rigour and real-world wisdom combined with a belief in the deeper purpose behind great leadership.

It's time for you to become a transformational communicator.

Transformational communicators with character and integrity are leaders who care deeply about people. They are driven to achieve purposeful, meaningful change in their organisation, community or society at large and use their communication skills to inspire, motivate and bring about positive change. They go far beyond the transactional communication style of conveying information and instead, focus on building relationships based on trust, respect and mutual understanding, because they understand that achieving anything truly great requires engaging hearts and minds around a compelling vision based on a desired shared future, and involving people in its creation.

It doesn't matter what role you play in life, transformational communication is a powerful communication approach for people in all kinds of positions to achieve extraordinary results.

Examples:

- An organisational leader who inspires their team to achieve a new benchmark in service by clearly communicating the vision and fostering a collaborative environment.
- A sports coach who motivates a sporting team to transcend limiting beliefs and perform at their best by helping them visualise the outcome, and by providing personalised support and encouragement.
- A teacher who encourages students to learn and grow by creating an engaging and supportive classroom environment and making it 'safe' for students to share and communicate their ideas and opinions.

In essence, transformational communication is a style characterised by purpose, empathy and authenticity, inspiring others to achieve their full potential while also moving the mission forward to achieve a lofty societal purpose.

This part of the book provides the practical blueprint to become a transformational communicator. It explores in depth the five steps of **The Transformational Communicator Method™** and gives you reflective questions and practical tools for each.

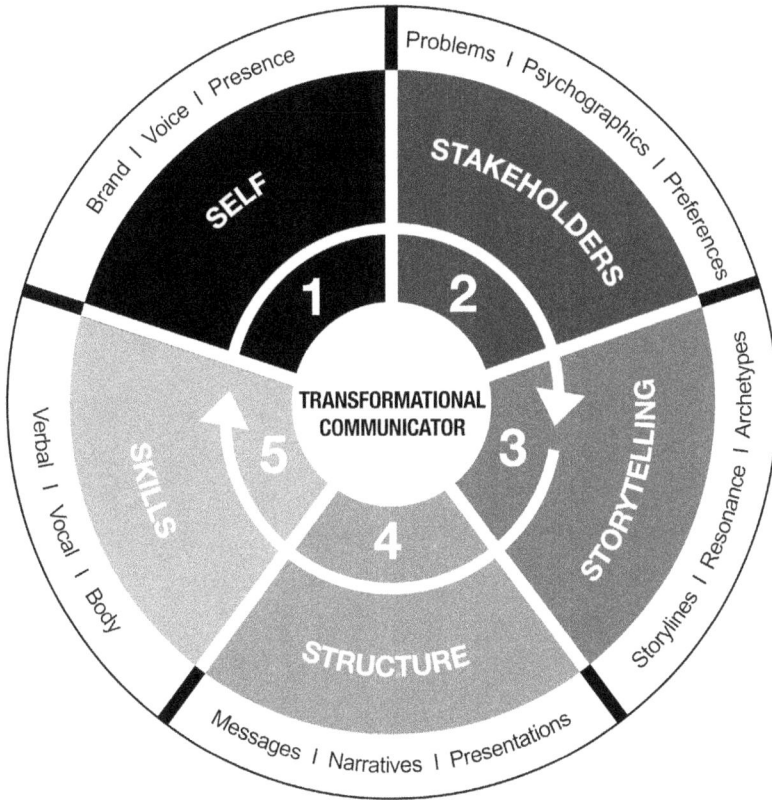

The Transformational Communicator Method™
©Ros Weadman

In summary, the five steps are:

1. Self

This step covers:

- building a strong personal brand
- defining your leadership voice
- cultivating your leadership presence

2. Stakeholders

This step covers:

- identifying your audience
- understanding your audience
- appealing to your audience

3. Storytelling

This step covers:

- the power of story
- why storytelling matters for leaders
- timeless story arcs
- archetypes for leadership storytelling
- types of stories every leader should tell
- micro stories: small in type, big in impact
- storytelling for influence
- seven pitfalls of leadership storytelling to avoid

4. Structure

This step covers:

- why structure matters
- strategic communication framework
- three-part messaging frameworks
- narrative structures that move people
- presentation frameworks that land impact
- frameworks for media messaging

5. Skills

This step covers:

- verbal language – crafting words for clarity and connection
- paralanguage – the voice of influence
- body language – speaking without words

By building your knowledge and applying the practical components of each of the steps, over time you will become the type of communicator who resonates deeply with your audiences. While the order of the steps is important because they build upon each other, you can also choose to focus on one particular step, or several steps at a time, depending on your current level of confidence and competence in each area, and based on your specific goals, needs and priorities.

The important thing is that you don't skip a step; that you cover them all. If, for example, you focus on storytelling without first clarifying your leadership vision and message, people may not fully understand or may be confused about what you're trying to achieve. And if you focus on storytelling first but don't know how to analyse your target audience's motivational drivers, again, your message may fall flat.

I recommend you first read the entire five steps, then go back to step one and work through each of the steps in order (self, stakeholders, storytelling, structure and skills). This will help you turn knowledge into skilful action through ongoing application and rehearsal.

Then, over time, watch your leadership communication become more influential and impactful. Your ability to nuance your message to different audiences and communicate effectively in a variety of situations and settings will build connection, trust and respect among your stakeholders, communities and followers. I've personally seen how becoming more confident and competent in leadership communication can enhance a person's career results, opportunities and impact.

Becoming a transformational communicator is not about faking it till you make it, either. It takes time, effort and energy to clarify your vision, craft your message, hone your verbal and body language skills, and cultivate a presence that conveys credibility and authority. But it's totally worth the investment of time and effort to complete all steps. Because an unclear message means people don't know what you stand for. An inability to frame and tell stories means you won't build trust and connection with audiences. And incongruent verbal and non-verbal skills means you'll confuse and disengage your audiences.

In the following pages, I outline the key components of each of the five steps, and provide clarifying questions and practical exercises to help you express and embody the techniques. So, stick with it because the day you can communicate your vision and message with clarity, confidence, conviction and credibility, is the day you can change the world.

2

Step 1: Self

'Knowing yourself is the beginning of all wisdom.'
Aristotle, Greek philosopher

Before trying to understand our audience or clarify our message, we must first seek to understand ourselves. Self-reflection is a powerful process that enables you to understand your strengths, uncover blind spots and adjust. Reflection is an opportunity to reflect on the past with openness and gratitude, and reflect forward with clarity and intention. And in so doing, advance professional development and performance. A study highlighted in the Harvard Business Review[1] of 442 executives asked to reflect on which experiences had the most impact on developing them as leaders, identified three key themes:

- surprise
- frustration
- failure.

The researchers found reflections that involved one or more of these themes proved to be the most valuable in helping the leaders grow. Surprise creates opportunities for questioning assumptions; frustration creates opportunities for innovative problem-solving; and failure creates opportunities to try something new.

Refection is an important part of this Self step. It helps you become more self-aware of your communication style and use the insights to clarify your vision and message and build your leadership brand.

This step covers building a strong personal brand, amplifying your leadership voice and developing your leadership presence.

Building a strong personal brand

The difference between brand and reputation

Everyone has a personal reputation but not everyone has a personal brand. It's a critical distinction to understand. Personal branding is a deliberate and strategic process of defining, expressing and leveraging an authentic self-identity for the purpose of distinguishing yourself from others.

Your personal brand is all-encompassing, embodying your identity, passions, values, beliefs, purpose, vision and expertise, which are invisible to the outside world. Together, these intrinsic elements influence the way people perceive you through your language, behaviour, messages, stories , public profile and performance results which are visible to the outside world.

The iceberg graphic illustrates the interplay between the invisible and visible elements of a personal brand.

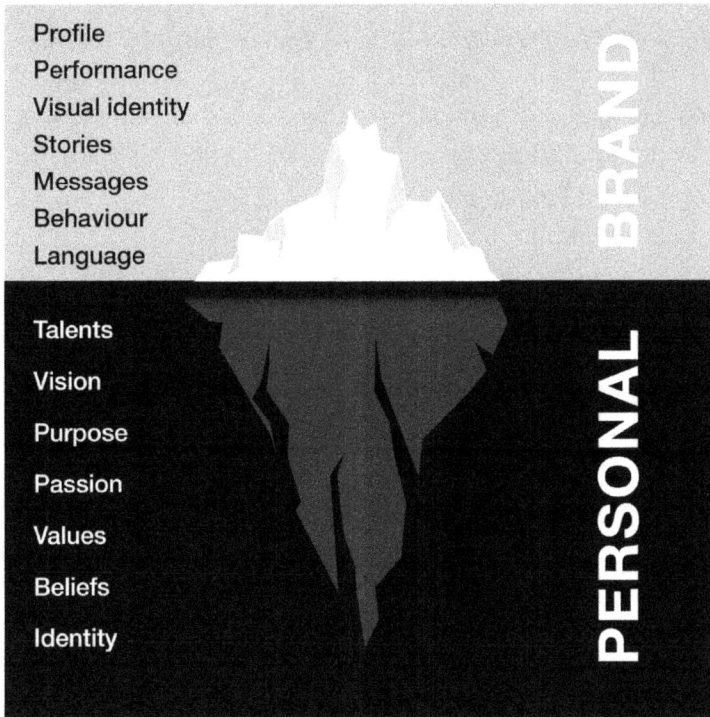

Personal brand iceberg
©Ros Weadman

Not everyone undertakes the deliberate and strategic process of personal branding. On the other hand, everyone has a personal reputation. From the first impressions you make to the way you communicate and the actions you take, people are always forming opinions and assumptions about you based on their direct or indirect experience with you.

Here's the rub. If you haven't taken control of your personal brand, your reputation as a leader is likely to be fragmented: differing from person to person. This means people could be confused about what you stand for as a leader.

The beauty of the personal branding process is that it builds you a more cohesive reputation. Over time, your personal brand and reputation become one and the same. This congruence between personal brand and reputation happens because you are showing up in the world – in person, online, on social media and in print – in a more aligned and consistent way.

Leaders with a strong personal brand shape their reputation by design rather than earning a fragmented one by default.

Why a personal brand matters for leaders

Building a strong personal brand benefits leaders in many ways. Here are six key benefits:

1. Purpose and meaning

Exploring your identity through the personal branding is a process of deep self-reflection which leads to a high level of self-awareness and strong sense of purpose. When you wake every day and feel connected to a worthy cause that inspires you, you will derive a strong sense of professional satisfaction and deep meaning from your work. Clarity of purpose enables you to think bigger picture and understand that your work makes the world a better place in some way.

2. Clarity and confidence

There's a sense of positive energy that's contagious when you're in the company of someone who is genuinely confident in their own skin and clear about who they are, what they stand for, how they make a difference and where they're heading. This is what the process of personal branding gives you. From the articulation of purpose, vision and values to the expression of identify, perspective and self-worth, personal branding gives clarity to make decisions and confidence to act.

3. Standing apart

Personal brands stand out; others blend in. In many service industries there's no shortage of service providers from whom to choose. But all things being equal, the professional leader who is clear about what they stand for, confident in their value and certain of their results, will stand out and have a competitive edge.

4. Authority positioning

An outcome of building a strong personal brand is becoming more well-known within your industry and broader networks. In a reputation economy, a strong personal brand accelerates the 'know, like, trust' process. Trust is the ultimate currency of business and workplace relationships and essential for building a great reputation. People want to hire, and do business with, people they trust.

5. Strategic partnerships

Having a strong personal brand enhances your ability to leverage partnerships. A strong personal brand can make you more attractive to potential strategic partners when there is an opportunity to enhance each other's service offering or advocacy for mutual financial benefit.

6. A more cohesive reputation

Have you considered people may perceive you differently to how you view yourself? If peoples' perceptions of you as a leader vary, you may have a reputation-reality gap problem. Sometimes we don't realise how we come across to others in different situations. Or we may show up inconsistently in different contexts so peoples' experiences of us varies. Building a strong personal brand is an effective way of creating a more unified perception of who you are. And closing the gap between your actual reputation and your desired reputation.

Five criteria of a strong personal brand

Building a strong, authentic personal brand doesn't happen in a vacuum. However, with intention, clarity, alignment, consistency and authenticity, you can leverage your personal brand in a most powerful way. Here's how:

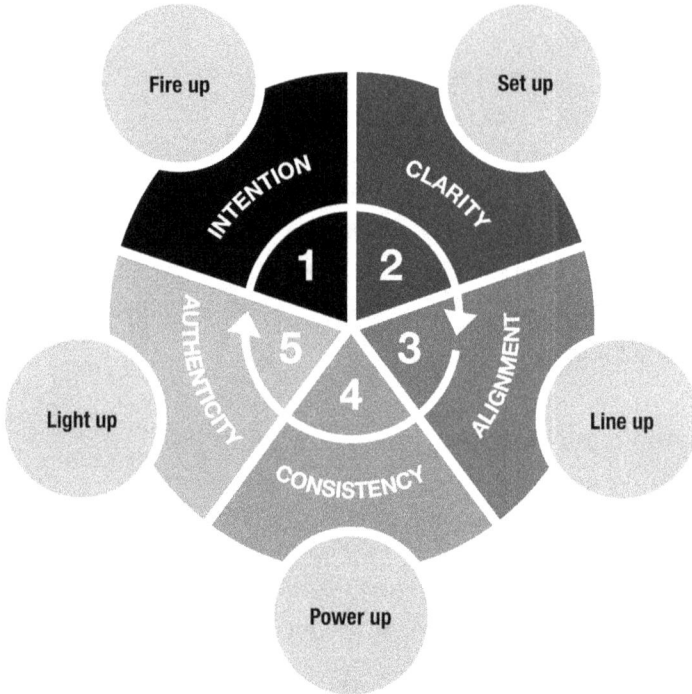

Five Criteria of a Strong Personal Brand
©Ros Weadman

1. Intention

It all starts with intention – a commitment to build a personal brand that reflects the kind of leader you want to be and to be known for. At the heart of this intention is a shift to adopting a personal brand mindset and all that goes with it, including the responsibility and accountability for what you think, say and do.

Intention sets in train decisions to gain clarity on your purpose, your beliefs and values, your message, your specialist value, your leadership style, your presence. In essence, how you intend to show up to the outside world. If you are intentional in all these areas, you'll build a strong personal brand and forge a desired reputation in the minds of those who matter to you and those you want to influence.

Brand is an inside job of which reputation is an external manifestation. Understanding that the principle of cause and effect applies to brand and reputation is an empowering concept for professionals to embrace. The fact that your brand is 100% within your control – from the values you uphold to the image you project, the messages you convey, the actions you take, the body language you use, the clothes you wear – puts you in the driver's seat of shaping how you would like to be perceived.

2. Clarity

The personal branding process helps you gain clarity on who you are, what you stand for and where you are heading as a leader. This clarity helps you identify and articulate a leadership purpose, values and vision, and shape how you want to be perceived, leading to more focused decision-making and purposeful actions.

Clarity of identity and a strong sense of self also gives a leader confidence in how they show up, certainty in their message and consistency in how they speak and act. This in turn, earns them trust and respect.

3. Alignment

People with a strong personal brand are committed to speak and act in alignment with their beliefs and values. This alignment gives them confidence, presence and influence. Think of political leaders, such as former New Zealand prime minister Jacinda Ardern or former

Finland prime minister Sanna Marin, for example. Although holding the country's most senior position, Sanna Marin stood firm on her belief to unapologetically express her youth, after a leaked video showed her dancing and singing with friends at a private function.

Similarly, Jacinda Ardern's belief in a compassionate and open communication style of leadership, rejecting the premise that prime ministers must be aggressive and masculine, became a beacon of what effective and modern political leadership looks like.

4. Consistency

Consistency builds visibility, trust and momentum. If you're consistent with your brand presence, online and in person, you're more likely to build a cohesive brand reputation because people gain a more unified understanding of who you are and what you're about. Consistency of brand presence also fosters trust with people because when you consistently make clear your unique character, qualities and capability, you cumulatively build a sense of familiarity, dependability and credibility in people's minds. Over time, consistency builds your public profile as your thoughts and ideas come more under the spotlight, with your message lighting up more of those around you.

5. Authenticity

What makes us individually different from each other is the secret sauce or X-factor of a personal brand. While intention, clarity, alignment and consistency are ways of being or habits that all people can embrace, authenticity is unique to everyone. No-one thinks, speaks or does things like you. It's your you-niqueness that ultimately sets you apart.

In other words, your personal brand is the authentic you. While you may think authenticity is a given when it comes to personal branding, unfortunately that's not always the case. In the world of people branding, the persona that someone projects may not always be their authentic selves.

Define your leadership purpose

Purpose is what we think about why we do what we do. A declaration of purpose reveals what a leader believes they're here to achieve; the worthy cause they have aligned themselves with and for which they want to make an impact.

It's not necessarily an easy or quick process to distil your leadership purpose to just a few powerful words, but once you land on it, it's worth the investment of your time and consideration.

To give you some inspiration, here are some purpose statements of some leaders I know:

- Two owners of a painting business are renowned for their punctual and precise painting prowess, and are also trailblazing a new path for women in trade industries by helping create a world where females are empowered, encouraged and confident to succeed. They've committed to '*leading by example and being positive role models for women in a traditionally male-dominated industry*'.
- An audiologist who runs a small business, is president of a women's business group and has founded several migrant support groups, has articulated a purpose of '*empowering people to access and optimise their inner strengths, enabling them to make the most of life's opportunities*.'
- My purpose as a small business owner is to '*empower human connection through communication that moves people*'.

Your leadership purpose is your 'why' and, in my experience, the most powerful 'whys' are an expression of love. If your leadership 'why' isn't an expression of love in some form, you may not have articulated your higher purpose. I'm not talking about the romantic kind of love but a version of love that improves people's lives or the planet in some way and moves humanity forward.

Love can be expressed in different ways through your 'why', depending on the contribution and impact you make on people's lives through your leadership. For example, your impact may be in the areas of:

- self-acceptance
- self-esteem
- connection
- community connectedness
- confidence
- belonging
- peace of mind
- optimism
- autonomy
- empowerment
- hope
- joy
- fulfilment
- health
- wellbeing
- healing
- gratitude
- forgiveness
- freedom
- resilience

To land on a 'why' that articulates a manifestation of love often requires asking the question, 'For what purpose?' several times. For instance, a physiotherapist may articulate their 'why' as 'helping people with mobility challenges to rebuild their physical strength and reduce their pain'. Here's how that why can chunk up a few notches by asking 'for what purpose?' several times:

1. For what purpose? *'So they can move their bodies more freely and function better in their everyday lives.'*
2. For what purpose? *'So they can regain their independence and confidence.'*
3. For what purpose? *'So they can reconnect with and do things that bring them joy and lead a more fulfilling life.'*

The third statement is a higher-purpose 'why' statement because reconnection, joy and fulfilment are expressions of self-love.

By articulating a leadership purpose statement that is aspirational in making a positive difference in the world provides a strong foundation from which to articulate your leadership vision and mission.

> **(?) Reflection questions**
>
> - Why did I want to become a leader?
> - What problem am I passionate about solving?
> - What is a just cause I can align my leadership with?
> - What am I passionate about in my leadership?

Articulate your leadership vision

Your leadership vision stems from your purpose and describes the kind of future you want to create as a leader. It provides a North Star, giving you clarity and direction on the difference you want to make in the world. A compelling vision guides you when making strategic decisions, such as which opportunities to say yes and no to, what knowledge and skills to develop, and what experiences to have so you can stride towards this desired future.

A clear vision also gives leaders an anchor when times get tough. When things go off track and risks you took don't pan out, or when obstacles get in the way, a clear leadership vision is like a lighthouse that helps you navigate rough seas and continue towards your destination.

Craft your leadership vision statement

In my work developing vision statements for leaders, I've found the most powerful vision statements have both an inward (self) and outward (others) focus. With this twin focus, a vision statement answers the question, '*what do I want to be known for as a leader*?'. And from a people/planetary perspective, it answers the question, '*what is the big picture difference I want to achieve as a leader*?'. This big picture difference is the legacy you leave as the result of your leadership work.

When the answers to these questions are combined, the vision articulates what the leader wants to achieve for themselves (inward focus) and what they want to achieve for the greater good (outward focus).

Professional vision - What do you want to be known for as a leader?

This question explores what you want to be known for in terms of your professional standing within your industry and what you want to be renowned for in terms of reputation. In other words, what level of influence and impact do you want to achieve within your field? What attributes do you want associated with your leadership brand when someone thinks of you or talks about you to others?

If you were able to shape your desired leadership brand in the minds of others, what would they say about you when you're not in the room? What three words would come up in the same sentence as your name?

When thinking about and writing down what you want to be known for, use these criteria:

- Write your responses in the first person ('I' and 'my' statements).
- Write it like it's already happened; so this future identity starts to filter into your subconscious.
- Write it so it can be measured; if it's too vague you'll have trouble conjuring a vivid picture and difficulty knowing when it's been achieved.

Here are some examples to spark your thinking:

- *'I am one of Australia's foremost experts on <insert industry category> and renowned for <insert specialist problem-solving expertise>.'*
- *'I am an accredited <insert practitioner status> working at the cutting edge of <insert profession> and renowned for <insert specialist problem-solving expertise>.'*
- *'I am the CEO of a global <insert industry type> company leading the world in the <insert problem-solving> space. As a leader, I am renowned for <insert leadership qualities/values>.'*
- *'I run one of Australia's top <insert profession> businesses. I am renowned for <insert specialist problem-solving expertise> among <insert niche or micro niche>.'*
- *'I am the owner of a <insert profession> practice and have a reputation for <insert specialist problem-solving expertise>.'*
- *'I am an in-demand global <insert profession> renowned for my work in <insert specialist area> with <insert niche or micro niche>.'*

- *'I am an internationally-recognised leader in <my industry> and renowned for my work in <insert specialist area>.'*

People / planet vision - What difference do you want to make?

The second part of a leadership vision describes the kind of future you want to create through your work. This externally-focused outcome is, in effect, an expression of optimism for a brighter future. It's about how you as a leader intend to create a ripple effect to change lives, to improve community outcomes, to move humanity forward in your role. It is, therefore, your mark on the world, your legacy.

For a business leader, their aspirational vision may describe the kind of future they want to create for their clients through the product or service they deliver. For a community leader, their aspirational vision may describe the kind of life they want to create for their constituents in the place they live.

When leaders make clear the difference they seek to make in the world through their vision, it helps their customers or followers understand what they stand for, and helps the teams they lead answer the question, 'why are we here?'.

When a leader articulates their legacy through a compelling vision they become a purpose-driven leader. Leaders with a compelling vision aligned with a higher purpose attract people into their sphere who resonate with this kind of future.

If you're looking for some inspiration for considering your leadership legacy, the United Nations' Sustainable Development Goals[2] are a good place to start. These goals, set in 2015 by the General Assembly of the United Nations, are a call to action by all countries to address global challenges related to poverty, inequality, climate, environmental degradation, prosperity and peace.

The 17 goals with 169 targets are designed to stimulate action to achieve transformational outcomes in key areas of critical importance for humanity and the planet by 2030. While there is an expectation that governments will take ownership and establish national frameworks to achieve these goals, there is much that individuals can do by their decisions and actions. The goals can be used to derive inspiration for articulating your leadership legacy.

Articulate the difference

When exploring the question of what difference you want to make, follow these criteria:

- Make it outward focused (for example, clients, other people, local community, environment).
- The outcome must solve a problem.
- Use optimistic language that is both aspirational and inspirational.

Here are some examples to spark your thinking:

- *'As a leader I've helped <audience> to overcome <insert problem> and <insert transformation>.'*
- *'Through my work in <specify work> I've helped x number of <insert client> to achieve <insert outcome>.'*
- *'As a <insert type> leader, my key impact has been in the area of <insert area> resulting in <insert result or ultimate outcome>.'*

Putting it all together

The next step is to combine the questions of *'what do you want to be known for?'* – your professional standing – and *'what difference do you want to make?'* – your planetary legacy – to craft your leadership vision statement.

As an example, here's my leadership vision:

'I am an Australian authority on leadership communication. My Transformational Communicator Method™ has helped more than one million leaders to communicate with purpose, power and presence so they can lead with greater influence and impact and create positive change in the world.'

Here are some more examples:

- *'I am a visionary leader in the area of <insert specialist area, industry>. Through my work in <insert work area> I've been able to achieve <insert outcome> which has helped <insert impact>.'*
- *'I am an internationally-recognised leader in <my industry> and renowned for my work in <insert specialist area>. My <insert signature methodology> is the cornerstone approach to <insert niche> and has helped more than one million people to <insert outcome>.'*
- *'I am the CEO of a global <insert industry type> company leading the world in the <insert profession> space. Through our research, we've helped more than one million people to <insert outcome>.'*
- *'I am an empathetic, transformational leader renowned for <insert relevant attributes>. I'm most proud or my work in the area of <insert specific area of work, project> which has directly resulted in <insert outcome, impact).'*

There are no real rules in crafting your leadership vision. As long as it is meaningful and inspiring to you, that's what matters most.

> **(?) Reflection questions**
>
> - What kind of world do I want to create through my leadership?
> - What big picture difference am I here to make?
> - What problems or challenges can I help solve?
> - How many people can I directly help?

Define your leadership values

Our core values dictate what we deem important and strive to uphold at all times. In our career and business life, core values are the guideposts by which we make decisions, determine priorities and take action. Examples of core values include stewardship, wisdom, accountability, growth, quality, integrity, service, excellence, culture, diversity, respect, empowerment, courage, generosity and community.

In conducting research for his book *Good to Great*[3], Jim Collins found that core values and purpose were essential for shifting from a company with good results to an enduring company of iconic stature, stating that, '*Enduring great companies preserve their core values and purpose while their business strategies and operating practices endlessly adapt to a changing world. This is the magical combination of "preserve the core and stimulate progress"*'.

When we speak and behave in line with our core values, we are more likely to feel happy and true to ourselves. However, if we say things and act in ways not congruent with our core values, we can feel unsettled and inauthentic. It can also affect our relationships with others who may perceive we've been fake or dishonest.

Making clear your core values is an important element of building a leadership brand. You want to be transparent with your core values so people know what you stand for. If, however, you act out of alignment with your core values with a colleague or client, you will lose credibility and trust and damage your reputation. That's why when determining your core values, ask yourself, 'What am I not prepared to compromise on, ever?'.

Embody your values

Core values expressed as actionable standards of behaviour make it easy for your colleagues and clients to know what to expect when working with you. This can include the expected approach to customer service, expected way of communicating, expected performance and so on.

Examples to spark your thinking

Here's some examples of how leadership core values can be turned into actionable statements:

- **Trust** – *'I do what I say I will.'*
- **Care** – *'I am kind and show empathy towards everyone.'*
- **Accountability** – *'I take full responsibility for my actions and follow through with others.'*
- **Relationships** – *'I put trust at the centre of all relationships because we are better together.'*
- **Integrity** – *'I am an honest and ethical leader who communicates transparently at all times.'*

When you turn your leadership core values into actionable statements, they become the yardsticks by which you think, speak and act. When applied consistently, these core values become the 'trademark behaviours' by which you are known and, ultimately, drive a strong and positive reputation for your leadership brand.

> **(?) Reflection questions**
>
> - What principles guide me as a leader that I'm not prepared to compromise on?
> - How do these principles translate into specific, actionable behaviours?
> - How can I better align what I say and do with my values?
> - How do I demonstrate each day that I'm living my core values?

Defining your leadership voice

Articulating your core message

While different issues and circumstances require different messages, every leader needs an overarching core message that underpins their leadership purpose and vision. Your core message is a stand-alone statement that deeply resonates with hearts and minds. That's because it makes sense in the context of what's happening in the world and it moves people to feel something deeply because it goes to the heart of their values, priorities and motivational drivers.

Your overarching core message could be a few words only, it could be a short phrase or it could be a sentence or two. It could be a call to action or describe the change or outcome you aim to create. Above all, it is a message of optimism and inspiration that uplifts people and becomes a beacon of hope. It's purpose is to be a catalyst for action.

A leader's core message is not only self-determining, it defines them as a leader. It's what they become known for because they embody it in everything they think, say and do. The leader is a messenger, with a powerful message to convey. However, it is important to understand that a message is not just what we say, but also how it is understood. A message is only a collection of words until an audience gives it meaning. If your message doesn't resonate with your audience, it won't land.

Here are some examples of leaders who had a bold, core message for the world:

- **Malala Yousafzai** – *'One child, one teacher, one book, one pen can change the world.'*
- **Mahatma Gandhi** – *'You must be the change you wish to see in the world.'*
- **Dr Martin Luther King Jr**. – *'I have a dream.'*
- **The Dalai Lama** – *'Be kind whenever possible. It is always possible.'*
- **Nelson Mandela** – *'It always seems impossible until it's done.'*
- **Jane Goodall** – *'What you do makes a difference, and you have to decide what kind of difference you want to make.'*
- **David Attenborough** – *'The future of humanity and indeed, all life on Earth, now depends on us.'*
- **Albert Einstein** – *'Imagination is more important than knowledge.'*
- **Leonardo da Vinci** – *'Simplicity is the ultimate sophistication.'*
- **Maya Angelou** – *'People will forget what you said… but people will never forget how you made them feel.'*
- **Oprah Winfrey** – *'Create the highest, grandest vision possible for your life, because you become what you believe.'*

My bold core message is, *'Leaders with a big vision and a bold message can change the world'*; it even has its own page at the start of the book. The reason it deserves to be heard is because in the current highly disruptive, volatile and uncertain world, humanity is becoming more divided and disconnected. We need transformational communicators to step up and galvanise hearts and minds around a big vision and a bold message for a desired future. Leaders of all institutions – business, government, media and not-for-profit need to hear it.

> (?) **Reflection questions**
>
> - What is my core message to the world?
> - Why does it deserve to be heard?
> - Who needs to hear it?

Craft your leadership narrative

Your leadership narrative conveys the essence of you as a leader and what you aim to achieve in your role. It's a tool for fostering two-way open dialogue, building rapport and trust, achieving your goals and driving change. Importantly, it helps people understand you better and know the 'why' behind the 'what' and the 'how'.

The below leadership narrative structure will guide you in developing your story. This six-step structure creates a powerful story arc that communicates who you are, what you stand for, the legacy you aim to leave and how you're going to get there.

The six steps are:

1. **Origin** – where you've come from
2. **Identity** – who you are
3. **Message** - what you stand for
4. **Vision** - where you're heading
5. **Impact** - the impact you intend to make
6. **Action** - how you go about it

To create your leadership narrative, work through the six steps below and use the two examples that follow as a guide.

1. Origin: where I've come from

Purpose: Identify relevant background factors and formative influences.

Question: *'What key life moments, milestones or experiences shaped me into who I am today?'*

- Defining moments, challenges or turning points
- Early influences or mentors (personal or professional)
- Key insights and lessons learnt

Example: *'I grew up watching my parents run a successful small business where every person was made to feel special; that taught me the value of empathy and service.'*

2. Identity: who I am

Purpose: Define core values and beliefs.

Question: *'What do I believe in deeply? What principles guide how I lead?'*

- Core values or principles (for example, courage, compassion, creativity, integrity)
- Beliefs that shape you (what assumptions you believe to be true)
- How you demonstrate your values through consistent behaviours

Example: *'I believe leadership is about empowering and uplifting others to achieve positive change, together. That's why I offer mentoring and support to our organisation's emerging leaders.'*

3. Message: what I stand for

Purpose: Articulation of a bold leadership message.

Question: *What is the core message that underpins your leadership?*

- Worthy causes or missions that drive you
- A message you have a strength of conviction for
- Public declaration of intent

Example: *'My manifesto is to create an organisational culture where everyone feels valued and understands why their work matters. We are better together.'*

4. Vision: where I'm heading

Purpose: Paint a clear picture of the desired future you want to shape.

Question: *'What change do I want to lead and aspire to achieve?'*

- Aspirational statement of intent
- Big picture difference for those whom you serve
- The legacy you want to create

Example: *'Together we are creating a future where our community is connected, vibrant and resilient, a future where every person belongs.'*

5. Impact: the impact I want to have

Purpose: Show how your leadership will create positive ripples.

Question: *'How will the world be a better place as a result of my leadership?'*

- The problems or challenges you want to solve
- Who benefits from your leadership and how

- Micro and macro impacts - industry, community, societal, global

Example: *'I want to empower emerging leaders to lead boldly and ethically, so that our impact is not just measured in actions but in values passed on.'*

6. Action: my purpose in action

Purpose: Articulate how you deliver on your purpose.

Question: *'What am I doing now and how do I invite others into the journey?'*

- Strategic organisational goals and priorities
- Current mission or project
- Inspiring others to join, contribute or support

Example: *'Right now, I'm championing a culture of belonging and inclusion in our organisation; not as a trend, but as a mindset and way of being.'*

Examples

Example 1: Leadership narrative of a government organisation CEO

Where I've come from

'I'm the daughter of a school teacher and a police officer; people who believed deeply in service to others. Growing up in a regional town, I saw firsthand the difference that accessible public services make in peoples' lives. That grounding has never left me.'

Who I am and what I stand for

'I believe that government leadership is ultimately about trust, earned through transparency, fairness and delivering on your brand promise. I'm passionate about embedding integrity into systems, and designing policies that are people-centric, not process-centric. My approach is to lead with empathy, rigour and a commitment to serving the greater good.'

Where I'm heading

'My vision is for public organisations to be responsive, inclusive and deeply connected to the communities they serve. Critical to achieving this outcome is transforming the sector's community engagement processes and embracing a mindset of trusting communities to be true partners in shaping services. Through this work, we'll pave the way to achieving our Community Vision for the benefit of future generations, together.'

The impact I want to have

'I want to leave behind a culture where courageous, empathetic and ethical leadership is the norm. Where every employee feels empowered to contribute, and every citizen feels heard. If people look back and say, 'They made government work better for people', then I've done my job.'

My purpose in action

'Right now, I'm focused on building cross-sector partnerships to help develop a new industry-wide approach to community engagement. I'm also mentoring emerging leaders to navigate complexity with confidence and care. Leadership in the public sector is not about being the loudest in the room; it's about being the most accountable. That's the standard I hold for myself, and the culture I strive to create.'

Example 2: Leadership narrative of a purpose-led business founder

Where I've come from

'I'm a former corporate manager turned entrepreneur. My turning point came when I almost experienced full burnout and realised how unsustainable our work culture had become. That experience pushed me to leave the comfort of a secure job and take the plunge to build something better.'

Who I am and what I stand for

'I believe all businesses should prioritise the health and wellbeing of their people over profits. It actually makes good business sense to do so. I'm passionate about creating workplaces where people are valued, treated with respect, and where purpose and performance coexist. As a founder, I lead by example to ensure my employees enjoy their work and stay energised.'

Where I'm heading

'My vision is to redefine success in business – people first, profit second. We're building a new platform that will help organisations measure not just how much they grow, but how well they care for their people, their communities and the planet. I'm building a company where our focus on employee wellbeing will be our competitive advantage.'

The impact I want to have

'I want to inspire a generation of founders and leaders to choose humanity over hustle. To empower them to prioritise mental health and wellbeing as an integral part of their business strategy and not just a nice-to-have. My greatest legacy won't be in revenue metrics; it will be in the ripple effect of the people and organisations we've helped transform.'

My purpose in action

'Right now, we're co-designing a new leadership program for founder-led teams. I'm also speaking more publicly about burnout and founder wellbeing because my personal experience provides valuable insights for others to learn from. If you want to build a successful business and want to do it without compromising your health and wellbeing or that of your staff, I'm here to show it's possible.'

(?) Reflection questions

- Where have I come from? – my story and defining experiences
- Who am I? – my values and beliefs
- What do I stand for? – my core message
- Where am I heading? – my vision for the future
- What impact do I want to have? – the micro and macro impacts along the way
- How am I demonstrating my purpose in action? – my current focus and invitation to others

Your leadership philosophy

Your leadership philosophy underpins and expands your core message. It reflects your deeply held beliefs.

Beliefs are the convictions or assumptions we hold to be true – about life, business or leadership – often formed over time through a mix of upbringing, experiences, education and cultural influence. For example, beliefs such as *'lying is bad'* or *'hard work always pays off'* are foundational ideas many people operate by, even if they've never explicitly articulated them.

In the context of leadership, your beliefs are likely shaped by your experiences in the workplace and the influence of mentors, role models or defining career moments. For instance, drawing on my own background in public relations and marketing, I hold the belief that *'purpose, core values and vision are necessary pillars of effective leadership communication'*. This belief informs the way I advise, write and lead.

Whether consciously or not, most leaders are philosophers. Over the course of our lives, we wrestle with ideas, test assumptions, challenge norms and defend what we believe in. From this intellectual and emotional inquiry emerges a personal leadership philosophy – a body of knowledge that becomes the lens through which we interpret the world and lead others.

In practice, this philosophy often manifests as a 'signature' approach. Consider how diverse philosophies influence professional disciplines:

- In medicine, one doctor may take a holistic, integrative approach while another adheres strictly to conventional protocols.
- In education, a teacher might centre their philosophy on experiential learning, while another prioritises discipline and structure.
- In financial planning, one advisor might focus on abundance thinking and values-based investment, while another focuses on prudence and conservative risk.

The same diversity exists in leadership. Some leaders prioritise innovation above all else. Others lead with empathy, inclusion, structure or performance. Your leadership philosophy is what sets you apart – it reveals what you stand for and guides how you respond to challenges, engage with people and shape your vision of the future.

Importantly, your leadership philosophy can become a magnet. When you speak it with clarity and act in alignment with it, you naturally attract people who believe what you believe. In this way, your philosophy becomes not just a personal compass, but a powerful influence strategy helping you build trust, rally support and inspire action.

Real-world examples

1. **Jacinda Ardern** – *'You can be strong and kind' philosophy*

   Former New Zealand Prime Minister Jacinda Ardern exemplified a leadership philosophy centred on empathy, inclusivity and service. Her belief that *'you can be both strong and kind'* underpinned her leadership approach and also her crisis communication approach, during the Christchurch mosque shootings and COVID-19, for example. She demonstrated that compassion is not a weakness but a strength that builds unity and trust. Her leadership showed how a clearly articulated and embodied philosophy could guide a nation through uncertainty with kindness at the core.

2. **Simon Sinek** – *'People don't buy what you do; they buy why you do it' philosophy*

   Author and leadership thinker Simon Sinek who made famous the 'Start with why' philosophy, built a movement around the belief that clarifying your 'why', linking what you do to a worthy cause, is a powerful way to lead because it attracts people who believe what you believe. His work has influenced thousands of leaders to reconnect with their deeper beliefs and lead from a place of purpose and conviction.

(?) **Reflection questions**

- What core belief guides your leadership?
- How has your leadership philosophy evolved through your career journey?
- In what ways can you more visibly live and lead by your philosophy?

Cultivating your leadership presence

Managing emotions and energy

Emotion is energy and every emotion has a frequency that creates a physiological response in our body. Our emotions and energy also cause physiological responses in others. For instance, when someone is angry, you might sense the 'heaviness' of the emotion in the room that causes people to feel anxious and disengage. Similarly, when someone is happy and joyful, you sense the 'lightness' of the emotion in the room that helps people feel at ease and open up. This is crucial for leaders to understand, not only because emotions can influence message receptivity but also because they can affect team morale, productivity and overall success.

Research shows emotions are, literally, contagious. '*Emotional contagion*' is the phenomenon where a person's emotional state and related behaviours influence another person's emotional state and behaviours, often without them even realising it. A simple example is when you smile at someone and they smile back or when you see someone yawn then you yawn or when someone laughs and it makes you laugh. It also extends to things like language, tone of voice, hand gestures and facial expressions. In effect, it's the automatic mirroring and synchronisation of emotions, leading to a shared emotional experience.

Research findings presented in a *Positive Psychology*[4] article in 2021 highlighted how positive and negative emotions have flow-on impacts in the workplace. A study in *Accident Analysis and Prevention* found that negative emotional contagion in the workplace led to more cognitive errors and workplace accidents. On the other hand, positive emotional contagion led to fewer cognitive errors and accidents.

The implications of emotional contagion for leaders is profound because their emotional state gives off a vibe, a mood, that can set the tone for a team or entire workforce, ultimately defining the organisational culture. We've all experienced meetings or workplaces where the energy of the leader or another person in the room impacted how everyone felt.

While the initial experience of emotions is often an automatic response to a situation or thought, how you react to, and engage with, those emotions is a choice. You can't always control what feelings arise, but you can choose how to manage and express them.

Emotional intelligence is now acknowledged as an essential attribute for effective leadership and this extends to leadership communication. Because leaders who communicate with a positive energy can inspire and motivate their teams, and foster a collaborative and productive atmosphere. Conversely, leaders who communicate with a negative energy and emotion, such as anger or frustation can create a toxic environment, leading to decreased engagement, increased stress and even high turnover rates.

> ## (?) Reflection questions
>
> - How does what I'm feeling right now impact my decisions and actions?
> - What are my common emotional patterns and what can I learn from them?
> - How can I better regulate my emotions in the future?
> - How does my emotional state impact those I work with?

Cultivating confidence

While competence is about what you can do, confidence is about what you believe you can do. And if you're confident in your own abilities, that feeling of self-assurance will help you perform the task to the best of your ability. As we know, when it comes to communication, not all leaders are confident when speaking to a large group or when under pressure, for example.

Confidence researchers Katty Kay and Claire Shipman determined that *'Confidence is the stuff that turns thoughts into actions'.*[5] As outlined earlier, through their studies they concluded that confidence is built through action. They also found that while confidence is part hardwired into your DNA, the brain can also rewire itself throughout life to cultivate confidence. Not by thinking positive thoughts all day long or faking it till you make it but by embracing mindfulness, rituals and habits; by dropping confidence killers, such as people-pleasing and perfectionism; and by taking more risks, being action-oriented and failing fast.

It makes total sense that action begets confidence. First take one step, then another and then another. This incremental process is also how you develop skills. So, to build your leadership communication confidence and skills, take action and watch your competence grow too.

(?) Reflection questions

- What am I most proud of accomplishing?
- How have my strengths shaped my impact?
- What steps could I take to build my confidence in leadership communication?

How the laws of influence affect presence

The likeability principle

A person's likeability can influence their success at work and in business. While that might seem like a 'Captain Obvious' statement to make, research into why this is the case has illuminated some interesting findings. For instance, Dr Robert Cialdini, in discussing the 'Liking Principle' in his book *Influence: The Psychology of Persuasion*[6], says that while we generally prefer to say yes to someone we know and like, this simple rule is used by total strangers to get us to say yes to them.

An example of this is the ever-popular Tupperware party. While it is the Tupperware representative who demonstrates the products and asks for the sale, research has shown that the strength of the social bond (likeability) between the party host and partygoers, is twice as likely to determine the product purchase (from the stranger) than preference for the product itself.

When it comes to leadership communication, the Likeability Principle can be used effectively to find common ground and build genuine rapport with people to facilitate agreement towards a particular outcome. For instance, to make a sale, to negotiate a contract, to adopt an idea, to illicit feedback, to engender a new behaviour, to sway a casting vote.

Building your leadership brand also accelerates the know, like and trust process. Because you are proactively positioning yourself, building a profile and shaping a cohesive reputation, people may feel they know you (and like you) before they actually meet you. The familiarity built over time from reading or listening to your content online, has created a perception of you without them even knowing you. And when they do finally meet you, the likeability factor comes home to roost.

A great piece of advice I received from one of my mentors was to *be easy to buy from and easy to work with'*. This advice goes to the heart of likeability; that is, being friendly, approachable, able to build rapport easily, having empathy and being personally relatable, are all attributes that make doing business with you a pleasure.

Factors influencing likeability

Social psychology researchers have found several elements contribute to someone being perceived as likeable. Body language, for example, can enhance or detract from likeability and the rapport-building process. For instance, crossing your limbs in a closed posture can discourage someone from striking up a conversation with you whereas using open gestures such as opening your arms to welcome someone into a group is more likely to result in people perceiving you more favourably.

Liking can also extend to how attractive we perceive someone to be. Social scientists refer to the 'halo effect' when one positive aspect of a person's physical appearance dominates the way people view them. Research shows if someone is viewed as attractive, we automatically assign them other positive attributes, such as talent, honesty, intelligence and kindness.

While physicality is a more 'superficial' factor in likeability, it does raise the important consideration of personal presentation and grooming, appropriate to the occasion. Professional image and styling is vital in cultivating an executive presence and fostering a leader's confidence. However, as it is a vast area of knowledge and one in which specialist expertise is recommended, I do not cover personal presentation and grooming in this book.

Similarity is another aspect that enhances likeability. Studies have shown this type of likeability generalises across areas, including opinions, personality traits, age, religion and lifestyle, such as having hobbies in common. Giving compliments and positive appraisal is another factor that leads to likeability.

> (?) **Reflection questions**
>
> - How am I focusing on earning the trust and respect of my colleagues?
> - In what ways do I demonstrate empathy and compassion in my leadership?
> - How could I be more proactive in building relationships?
> - How can I cultivate my executive presence?

The authority principle

Authority isn't just about title, it's about positioning; how you are perceived by others. Did you know you can't not influence? What you say and what you do influences people's perceptions of you; however, what you *don't* say and *don't* do also shapes people's perceptions of you. An example I used earlier is if you don't return someone's phone call or email for two weeks, the not saying and the not doing speaks volumes.

Knowing that our actions and non-actions influence people's perceptions of us, it makes sense to influence with intention. The authority principle – another of Dr Robert Cialdini's six laws of influence – can help you position yourself as an authority in your industry.[6]

Some ways you can use the authority principle to reinforce your leadership presence:

- Dress for success because first impressions matter even in an increasingly online marketplace and hybrid workplace. Being well groomed, with hair, clothing and accessories that align with your personal style, gives you that extra spring in your step from feeling confident and purposeful.
- Trademark any intellectual property you develop, including creative work, such as logos and illustrations, taglines, names of products and signature models and methodologies.
- When guest speaking, provide a biography and speech introduction blurb that positions you as an authority in your industry. Rather than sounding like a resume, a biography includes what makes you different from others in the field and why your message matters in the world, now.
- Use open body language to project confidence and certainty. Closed body language, such as crossed arms and legs and not looking straight at the audience give an impression of uncertainty and lacking confidence.
- When speaking, use 'command tonality'. This is when there is a downward inflection at the end of a sentence, so it sounds more direct and emphatic. Questioning tonality, on the other hand, has an upward inflection. This sounds like you are seeking validation of your statement and can give the impression you are uncertain of your content.
- Include accreditations, qualifications and awards on your website and marketing material.

? Reflection questions

- Am I presenting myself in the way I want to be perceived?
- When I speak, do I convey confidence or unconfidence?
- Do my team members have a genuine willingness to follow my guidance?
- How am I potentially undermining my own authority right now?

Step 2: Stakeholders

'The most basic of all human needs is the need to understand and the need to be understood. The best way to understand people is to listen to them.'
Dr Ralph Nicholls, 'Father of listening'

When communicating, we're often focused on sending our message and not so much on how it will be received. However, what Dr Ralph Nichols found out about the importance of listening underscores the importance of two-way communication. Before his 40-year pioneering work in the field of listening, Dr Nichols began his career as a high school speech teacher and debate coach. He found that as his debaters improved their listening skills, their persuasive skills also improved.

Imagine what kind of world we would have today if some of our leaders were better listeners? People on both sides of a debate, conflict or issue, would understand each other better. Creating opportunities for two-way dialogue is a core component of transformational communication.

In this step, we consider three critical factors that help us build trust and connection with stakeholders, including identifying your audience, understanding your audience and appealing to your audience.

Identifying your audience

Audience segmentation

Leadership communication isn't just what you want to say; it's how your message is received that matters. Much time is spent crafting the perfect message. Not enough time is spent understanding the audience – their beliefs, values, fears, aspirations and the like. Because if your message doesn't resonate with the target audience, it is a wasted opportunity to advance your goals and priorities.

When planning a communication about a topic or issue, the first step is to identify the audiences who need to be communicated with. Often there is more than one audience. In fact, there's often many audiences – internal and external stakeholders.

The key point to understand is that a one-size-fits-all message doesn't usually work. One simple key message is fine if you are dealing with a fairly homogeneous audience but when you have a more complex issue or multiple stakeholders with differing needs, perspectives and situations, you need to tailor your message for each group. The message needs to be nuanced to the audience.

To understand what each of your audiences needs to hear and how they prefer to consume it, you need to go through a process called 'audience segmentation'. This involves identifying audiences by type then mapping each audience in terms of their demographics (statistical characteristics of a group, such as age, gender, income level, educational level) and psychographics (psychological and emotional characteristics of a group, such as concerns, beliefs, values, fears, attitudes and aspirations). I go into psychographics in more detail in the next section.

Segment by distinct groups

Distinct stakeholder groups – both internal and external – are those specific individuals and groups you want to target for your communication. For a local council organisation for example, internal stakeholders are executives, councillors, employees and volunteers. External audiences might include residents, businesses and community groups. For a business, internal stakeholders would include the board, executives and employees, and external stakeholders would include customers, investors and social media followers.

Segment by hierarchy

Another way of segmenting audiences is by primary, secondary and tertiary audiences.

A primary audience is the main target group to whom the message is directed. They are the direct beneficiaries or groups directly impacted by a decision, event or situation. They may also be the group that has the highest interest in, or power of influence on, a particular topic. Because of this, they are the most likely to engage in the issue.

A secondary audience is a group not directly affected by the issue or at least not to the same degree as the primary audience but still have a level of interest or influence.

A tertiary audience is one step further removed from the secondary audience. Although these groups are not directly impacted, they are still important, because they may still have a level of influence in the decision-making process that impacts the final outcome.

Just as a primary audience has a message developed especially for them, so too, secondary and tertiary audiences need a message relevant to them. As an example, suppose a rural council adopted an advocacy plan to seek government funding to help build a new aquatic facility to replace the old aquatic facility demolished in a significant flood event.

In a scenario where the council wants to communicate its plan to pursue government funding, the audiences could be segmented as follows:

- **primary audience** – local township residents for whom the pool is for
- **secondary audience/s** – specific state and federal government departments
- **tertiary audience/s** – local members of parliament; broader community

On the other hand, in the same scenario but where the council wants to speak directly to the government, the audiences could be segmented as follows:

- **primary audience** – specific state and federal government departments
- **secondary audience/s** – local residents
- **tertiary audience** – local members of parliament; broader community

Reflection questions

- Who, specifically, needs to hear my message most – primary audience?
- Who else needs to hear my message – secondary audience?
- And who else needs to hear my message – tertiary audience?

Understanding your audience

Identify problems and pain points

The purpose of a product or service is to solve a customer problem – to meet a need, address a challenge, alleviate a pain point, fulfil a desire or satisfy a want. In effect, customers are looking for the right product or service to take them from where they are now (stuck in their problem) to where they want to be in the future (their problem is solved).

Customers of government organisations also have problems or pain points they want resolved. For instance, residents living on a busy road where there have been many car crashes want their local council to fix the problem by making the road safer. Or, residents living in a country town without many facilities or activities to engage young people want the local council to resolve the problem by building a skate park. Or, residents who have experienced a natural disaster and lost their home need financial and other support from the federal or state government to help them get back on their feet.

When, as a leader, you can articulate the distinct value of the solution you provide that solves a problem, you will connect with your target audience in a very powerful way. As you dive deeper into understanding their motivations, desires and frustrations, the clearer it becomes that it is the *value* of the solution – rather than the actual product, service or project itself – they are really buying or buying into. That is, how effectively the proposed solution will take them from where they are now in their current state of having a problem or a pain point of some kind, to their desired aspirational future state of having their problem solved or pain point alleviated.

So, before crafting a message or narrative for a situation, take time to fully understand the problems and pain points your stakeholders are experiencing, and the alternative future they deeply desire. Because to understand the true value of your idea or proposed solution to stakeholders, you need to first consider the situation from their perspective.

Define what your audience cares about

Demographics, while important, are often not as important as the psychographic factors that drive human motivation and behaviour. So, to understand a target audience deeply, we need to consider their thoughts and feelings about an issue. This is where psychographic analysis comes in.

Psychographics is about considering an audience based on their shared psychological characteristics, such as values, attitudes, interests and aspirations. Knowing this information is critical so a leader can frame and deliver their message in a way that resonates with the audience.

Here's an example of how understanding audience psychographics works. In 2023, I was involved in an advocacy campaign seeking to influence the federal government's intended water reforms. The reforms sought to reintroduce water buybacks – a program where the government purchases water from irrigators – as part of its plan to return more water to the Murray Darling Basin.

Many local councils across Australia joined forces with their local businesses, industry groups, farmers and many citizens in a concerted effort to stop this part of the water reform from going through the parliament. While acknowledging the importance of protecting the environment, the councils and their ally stakeholders all shared a concern, a belief, a worldview that water buybacks was not the answer to the problem. They were concerned that water buybacks would negatively impact their businesses, local economies and communities like it had done several years earlier. In effect, the council leaders galvanised the hearts and minds of the key stakeholders around the things that mattered most to them – their shared beliefs, values, concerns and fears around their lives and livelihoods as well as the environment on which they valued and depended.

Identify core needs

Like beliefs, fears and concerns, understanding the core needs of a target audience is another valuable way of understanding audience psychographics; it illuminates what motivates people and drives their behaviour. I use Maslow's Hierarchy of Needs model to understand the motivational drivers of target audiences, so I know how to frame a message that taps in to what an audience is thinking and feeling right now about a particular issue in the current context of their world.

Maslow proposed that all individuals have a basic set of needs they strive to fulfil. The five-part model has the most fundamental of human needs at the bottom of the pyramid, being physiological needs for food, water, shelter and the like. The needs rise through to higher emotional needs to the need for self-actualisation, achieving one's full potential, at the top, as humans strive to become better versions of themselves.

Below is a brief explanation of the five core needs:

- **Physiological** needs – basic needs for survival, such as water, food, air, shelter, sleep
- **Safety/security** needs – a need to feel safe and have stability, such as having a secure property, job, life, community, future
- **Love/belonging** needs – a need for social connection, friendships, relationships and a sense of belonging
- **Esteem** needs – a need for self-esteem, recognition, respect, achievement, significance, pride, contribution
- **Self-actualisation** needs – a need for personal growth and fulfilment, to reach one's full potential

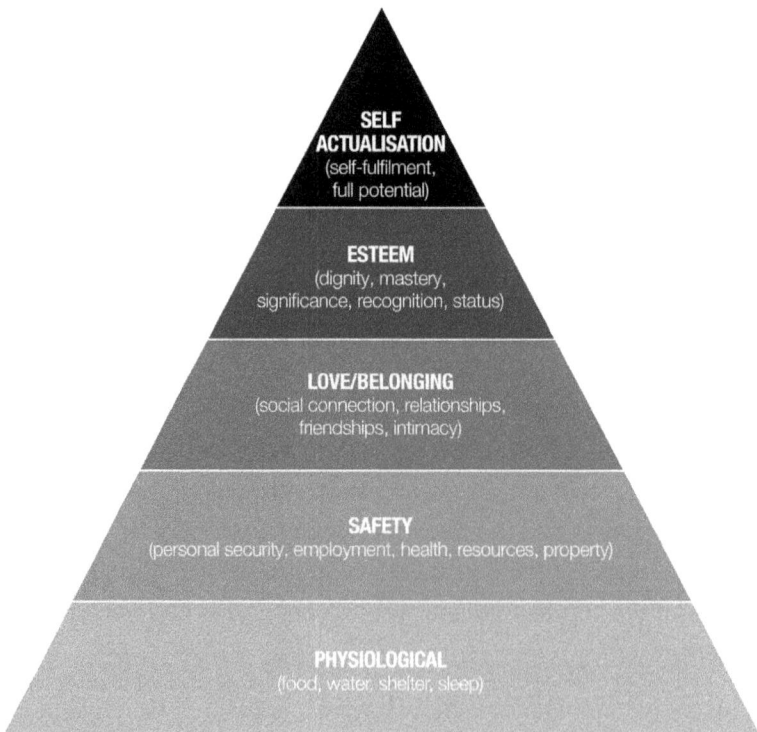

Maslow's Hierarchy of Needs

Maslow believed humans first seek to satisfy the lower order physiological and safety needs because they are essential to survival. Humans then move up the hierarchy in a systematic way, seeking to satisfy the higher order psychological needs.

For target audience analysis, the idea is to understand the exact core need your target audience is trying to satisfy and where your product, service or solution fits in to the hierarchy. You can then design your message to appeal to one of these motivational drivers in a meaningful way. The more closely aligned the target audience need is to your proposed solution, the more likely your message will resonate.

Here's how you can apply the model in understanding target audience motivational drivers. Let's say a local council wants to introduce a new local law in relation to responsible dog ownership. They've tightened the rules about having dogs on a lead following a spate of dog attacks at parks where children play. When crafting their core message and narrative, the core need they need to tap into is the need for safety. In other words, the message needs to be anchored on how the new local law will enhance neighbourhood safety and help prevent potential future dog attacks.

Similarly, if a local council wishes to embark on a campaign with the aim of getting more people in the community to volunteer to deliver 'meals on wheels' to people's homes, then they could frame their message and narrative around two core needs: 1) esteem, to appeal to a person's need to feel proud and significant from participating in such a worthy cause, and 2) self-actualisation, to appeal to a person's need for personal growth and seeking more meaning in their life.

When considering any target audience, taking time to identify the various psychographic factors at play, including beliefs, concerns, aspirations and core needs, will put you in a good position to understand a situation from their perspective and craft your message accordingly.

> **(?) Reflection questions**
>
> - What does my target audience believe about the problem or pain point?
> - What concerns or fears keep them awake at night?
> - What core needs are they seeking to be fulfilled?
> - What do they aspire to achieve in the future?
> - How would my target audience define success?

Map the emotional journey

Problems and pain points are part tangible and part emotional. For example, residents living in a small town without enough facilities and activities to engage young people may experience a problem of increased petty crime in local neighbourhoods (tangible) and this makes them feel anxious and fearful (emotional).

The bigger the problem, the greater the need or the more troubling the pain point in the mind of the stakeholder, the higher the value the stakeholder will place on finding a solution. This is because the person is motivated to seek relief from the mental unease, tension or discomfort they are feeling caused by the problem or pain point, and they want to move towards a place of comfort and internal equilibrium.

Resolved problems and pain points are also part tangible and part emotional. For example, if the small-town community lobbies their local council and they agree to fund a new skate park for young people and to remove the graffiti at no cost (tangible), this makes them feel happy and gives peace of mind (emotional).

The difference between the problem state and problem-resolved state is a gap. To articulate the true value of your proposed solution to stakeholders, you must articulate how the package of benefits of your solution closes the gap between the stakeholder's current state and their desired future state – that is, how it will take them from A to B, as shown below.

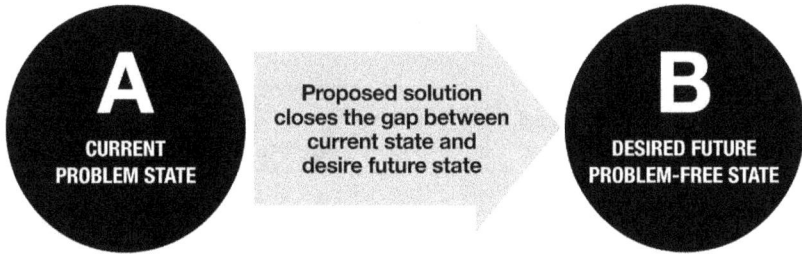

The stakeholder's acceptance of your idea or solution as the bridge that could close gap will come down to how well you position the solution in their mind through your messaging and storytelling.

Mapping the stakeholder's emotional journey

The below table shows a worked example mapping the logical and emotional factors of both the current problem state and desired problem-free state. This information provides a solid foundation upon which to craft a message that aligns with your goal; in this example, to create a safe neighbourhood and alleviate a major problem or pain point for the stakeholder.

Example of mapping a stakeholder's current state and desired future state:

CURRENT STATE		PROPOSED SOLUTION	DESIRED FUTURE STATE	
Stakeholder problem: Cars speeding along local road		(package of benefits)	Problem-free state: Cars no longer speeding along local road	
Tangible factors	Emotional factors	Proposed solution	Tangible factors	Emotional factors
Cars travel at up to 80km in a 50km zone Increased safety risk to traffic and pedestrians Three traffic incidents in last six months	Residents feel anxious about more potential crashes Parents fear their children may get hit by a car	At a townhall meeting the council informs the community it will install traffic-calming treatments, including signage, three speed humps and two chicanes, within the next three months at no cost to ratepayers. They will conduct an education campaign to inform the local community and driving public.	Traffic slows to between 30-50km Lowered risk of traffic accidents	Residents are happy Parents have peace of mind that their children can continue riding their bikes to school

The next step is to define and refine the complete package of benefits of your proposed solution so you can articulate a message that will resonate with stakeholders.

> ## ? Reflection questions
>
> - What tangible factors define the current state for the target audience?
> - Which emotions does the current state trigger in the target audience?
> - What tangible factors would define the desired future state?
> - How would the target audience feel once the problem or pain point is resolved?

Appealing to your audience

Appeal to preferences

Channel preferences

Diverse audiences require diverse channels because we all have preferences for how we want to be communicated with and how we want to consume information. Chosen channels must also consider the context and specific circumstances surrounding a leader's communication.

For example, in 2023, I developed a communications strategy connected to the recovery phase of a natural disaster, a flood event that inundated hundreds of homes in multiple towns. As a result, hundreds of families were displaced and had to find alternative temporary accommodation while their homes could be repaired and, in some cases, rebuilt. Some people stayed with friends or relatives, while many lived in a caravan, shed or other structure.

We were not only communicating with people who were uprooted from their homes, we were dealing with people and whole communities suffering mental health and wellbeing challenges from the trauma they had experienced, and the ongoing struggles and frustrations of having their lives and livelihoods turned upside down.

In this situation, social media was not the right medium to reach these people. Communicating face-to-face through community leaders, agencies and council community development workers, along with using printed materials were the best conduits for information for a long time. Social media was still ok for broader reach. This example highlights that context often dictates audience preference.

Leaders of organisations also need to consider whether their organisation's digital-first approach is inadvertently undermining their communications. While using digital channels are a key part of the distribution mix, I've seen some government organisations keep whole stakeholder groups in the dark because of an over-reliance on, or obsession with, digital communication. Or, using digital communication only because it's quick and less resource-intensive.

Just because a message was posted on social media, uploaded to a website or sent via an email newsletter, doesn't mean the job is done. Oftentimes, traditional forms of communication, such as human-to-human or printed materials, are the most appropriate, relevant and desired conduits, depending on the needs, preferences and circumstances of the audience.

That's why an 'audience-first' communication approach is better than a' digital-first' communication approach because audience-first doesn't just do what's cheap and easy, it takes account of the target audience:

- demographics
- psychographics
- language preferences
- information consumption habits.

The inherent heterogeneity of audiences means that an integration of both digital and traditional forms of communication is most often needed to optimise reach and engagement. In today's communications-technology-driven world, the mantra, 'diverse audiences require diverse communications' still applies.

> ## (?) Reflection questions
>
> - What are the typical communication channels of choice of my target audience?
> - What are the best communication channels to use, having regard to the situational context?
> - What is the best mix of communication channels to ensure we reach the target audience?

Communication preferences

People have different communication styles. Some want the big picture, some want the detail, some want both. There are several personality and behavioural profiling tools available, such as DISC®, that reveal a person's attributes, including their communication styles. Understanding the different communication styles gives you insight into how others perceive you as a leader and helps you adapt your style so you can optimise interactions with others. In other words, foster two-way dialogue not just one-way communication.

For example, the DISC® tool classifies people into four types - D for 'dominant' types, I for 'influence' types, S for 'steady' types and C for 'compliance' types. Understanding these four types provides a window into people's communication priorities, how these priorities influence their behaviour and how people prefer to be communicated with.

Research[7] shows that implementing this tool across an organisation to learn about the various work styles and communication preferences of employees can increase workforce productivity. A study on the implementation and effectiveness of the profiling tool in sport management and sport coaching classrooms at the university level also suggested that such behavioural profiling tools and activities can enhance self-awareness and help develop leadership skills.[8]

The below table summarises the four DISC® types.

C – Compliance	D - Dominance
• C types are precise, logical, careful, formal, disciplined, detailed • Driven by the need to be right (correct) • Greatest fear is criticism of their work • Wants facts, research, proof, reasoned logic, details	• D types are decisive, blunt, strong-willed, competitive, demanding, assertive • Driven by the need to win • Greatest fear is loss of control • Wants the big picture, directness, outcomes, and they want it fast
S – Steadiness	I - Influence
• S types are steady, careful, patient, trustworthy, cooperative and modest • Driven by a need to be comfortable • Greatest fear is loss of stability • Wants order, certainty, calmness, no sudden changes, process	• I types are sociable, talkative, open, enthusiastic, energetic and persuasive • Driven by a need to be liked • Greatest fear is social rejection • Wants inclusiveness, focus on relationships, positive atmosphere

When a leader communicates in a way that appeals to the communication preference of the audience, there is the potential for greater understanding and greater success of communication outcome. When a leader addresses a larger audience with a mix of communication styles, the best approach is to weave through language that appeals to all four types. Give the big picture but also give the detail.

The *'Tell me the time; don't build me the clock'* maxim reminds us to get to the point and not waffle in our communication. 'Telling the time' is communicating the main points only, such as the 'what' and 'who'. Whereas 'Building the clock' is communicating all the other details too, such as the when, where, why and how.

D types will more likely appreciate the 'tell me the time' approach, and S and C types are more likely to prefer the 'build me the clock' approach. S types need enough information to feel safe and comfortable while C types need the detail so they can satisfy their need for reasoned logic and proof.

While often leaders just want the main point or a situation requires it, the details can give critical understanding for more balanced decision-making. I encourage professionals to prepare their message for both 'telling the time' and 'clock-building' scenarios, then use one or both, as appropriate.

- For 'telling the time', deliver a succinct, self-contained statement that gives the bottom-line impact of the issue (the 'what'). By self-contained, I mean the statement makes sense on its own without the need for questioning.
- For 'clock building', wrap the why, how and other details into an engaging story. This can be how you concluded the 'what' or a case study that illuminates the impact of the 'what'.

At your next meeting, start by 'telling the time', then, if appropriate, 'build the clock'. By preparing for both scenarios, you can adapt your communication to suit the occasion.

> **(?) Reflection questions**
>
> - What is the communication preference of the person I'm talking to?
> - How can I adapt my own communication style to ensure this conversation is two-way?
> - How can I build language and imagery into my presentation that will appeal to the four communication styles?

Sensory preferences

We experience the world through our senses so it's not surprising that they can impact how we communicate. In everyday language we use words associated with our senses – vision, hearing, taste, smell and touch – because this is how we, as humans, process information. Most often, people will prefer one sense over another, and this can influence our preferred language type.

- People with a strong **visual orientation** use words associated with seeing (*'I see what you mean'*).
- People with a strong **auditory orientation** use words associated with hearing (*'I hear what you say'*).
- People with a strong **kinaesthetic orientation** use words associated with touch or emotions (*'I feel I understand you'*).
- People with a strong **gustatory orientation** use words associated with taste (*'That leaves a bitter taste in my mouth'*).
- People with a strong **olfactory orientation** use words associated with smell (*'I smell a rat'* or *'Something smells fishy'*).

As with communication styles, while you can't know the sensory preferences of an entire audience, if you choose words that appeal to the different sensory modalities, you'll have a greater chance of appealing to more people within the target audience.

(?) **Reflection questions**

- What is my preferred sensory preference and how does this potentially bias my communication?
- How can I adapt my language so my message is more receptive to the person I'm talking to?
- How can I build language and imagery into my presentation that will appeal to all the sensory preferences?

4

Step 3: Storytelling

'The most powerful person in the world is the storyteller. The storyteller sets the vision, values and agenda of an entire organisation.'

Steve Jobs (1955-2011) – co-founder of
Apple and Pixar Animation Studios

Storytelling is fundamental to how we as humans connect, learn and make sense of the world around us. Stories allow us to share information and experiences, and they are an important vehicle for transmitting cultural traditions, morals and values.

For leaders, stories are a powerful means for sharing their goals and plans, and for bringing the vision to life through vivid imagery and evoking emotions. Importantly, they are a powerful tool for building rapport, trust and connection, and motivating and inspiring others towards a common mission.

In this step, I cover topics to help leaders understand the power of storytelling, timeless story arcs, storytelling archetypes, the types of stories they should tell and storytelling pitfalls to avoid.

The power of story

Stories are central to our daily lives. Our conversations are based in story. We read books and magazines. We watch movies. We listen to music. We engage with social media. Almost everything we convey and consume is based in story. And that's not surprising; we're wired for it – story is in our DNA!

Our love of, and fascination with, story was ignited by fire. Anthropologists trace storytelling back thousands of years to when humans began to control fire. Fire not only kept people warm, safer from predators and enabled the cooking of food; it also sparked social interaction because fire extended the day beyond the survival requirements of hunting and gathering.

In groundbreaking research on the hunter-gatherer bushmen of southern Africa, anthropologist Polly Wiessner found major differences between day and night talk. She found that daytime talk focused on practicalities, complaints and gossip while, '*Night activities steer away from tensions of the day to singing, dancing, religious ceremonies, and enthralling stories, often about known people.*[9] Importantly, storytelling built rapport among people as they shared stories of their culture, rituals and traditions.

Stories change our brains

Modern day research has built on Weissner's findings with neuroscientists finding that stories actually change our brains. Neuroscientists talk about 'neural coupling' or 'neural synchronisation' – the syncing of our brains so we're on the same wave length. When someone listens to a story, their brain neurons fire in the same patterns as the speaker's brain.

Listening to stories also make our brains release certain hormones. For instance:

- Cortisol and adrenaline, the stress hormones, are released when there is pressure, danger or risk involved and that makes people pay attention.

- Oxytocin, the love hormone, is released when someone tells a personal story. The audience leans in to the storyteller and this fosters connection, empathy and trust.

- Endorphins, feel good hormones, are released when there is humour or a joke is told as part of a story.

Story as a vehicle for behaviour change

Stories aren't just for information or entertainment purposes, they're used to impart meaning about different issues and encourage people to think, feel and act differently. Public education and prevention campaigns designed to create attitudinal or behavioural change are examples of this.

The grim reaper advertising campaign during the AIDS epidemic of the 1980s and the many road safety campaigns over decades come to mind of how storytelling has been used to instil the emotion of fear as a way of getting people to change their behaviour.

Government road safety and drink-driving campaigns, for example, have used this kind of fear-inducing storytelling for this purpose. Through strong visual imagery on a television commercial showing the dangers of speeding drivers, motorcyclists weaving in and out of traffic, cyclists not obeying traffic signals and all ending up getting hurt or hurting others. These stories, although told in around 30 to 60 seconds, pack a punch with their strong and memorable messages, such as 'If you drink and drive, you're a bloody idiot'.

Similarly, the photographs of a cancerous lung and gangrenous feet on cigarette packaging tell a powerful story without words. The imagery is so stark and compelling that the mind can use its imagination to surmise that people who smoke too much can end up like this.

Such graphic advertising almost always go hand in hand with support campaigns to help people who make the decision to change their behaviour.

Why storytelling matters for leaders

The fire-story tradition continues. The tradition of gathering around fire to bond and connect with each other continues today around the world in many guises:

- restaurants create candlelit dinners to encourage intimate conversations
- families and groups of friends sit around fire pits and campfires to bond
- in workplaces, employees gather to hear the CEO's fireside chat.

Storytelling plays a big role in corporate environments today because it's recognised that storytelling:

- strengthens employee connection and engagement
- creates shared meaning around organisational purpose, values and goals
- passes on traditions, rituals and behaviours
- is a powerful force for driving the desired brand narrative and shaping brand identity.

Virgin Group founder Richard Branson embraced the power of fire and storytelling. In 2015, he commissioned an artist to handcraft a 'fireball' for his team to gather round and brainstorm at his home on Necker Island. Branson uses fireside storytelling for visioning about the future with his team.

Whether it's driving major change or framing stories for media, internal communications, speeches or public presentations, storytelling is a key strategic leadership communication tool for building trust and connection.

Timeless story arcs

Aristotle's three-part plot structure

We have Aristotle to thank for giving us the basic formula for storytelling when he stated that all plots should be structured logically, with a beginning, middle and end. He emphasised the cause and effect relationship of events that create a logical sequence for a plot.

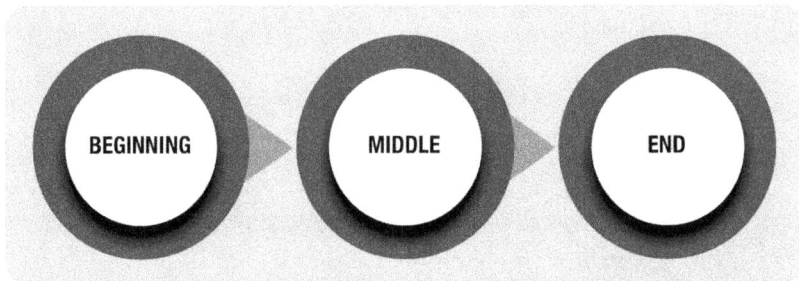

Aristotle's foundational framework is the basis of what we now call the three-act structure used in screenwriting and other storytelling fields across the globe.

The three-act structure

The three-act structure provides a framework for a chain of events that correspond to the beginning, middle and the end of a situation. The framework moves from an initial state of equilibrium to a state of disruption then to a new state of enhanced equilibrium.

The three acts comprise of Act I (the set up), Act II (the confrontation) and Act III (the resolution). Note that the three acts can neatly overlay Aristotle's three-part plot structure as shown in the below model.

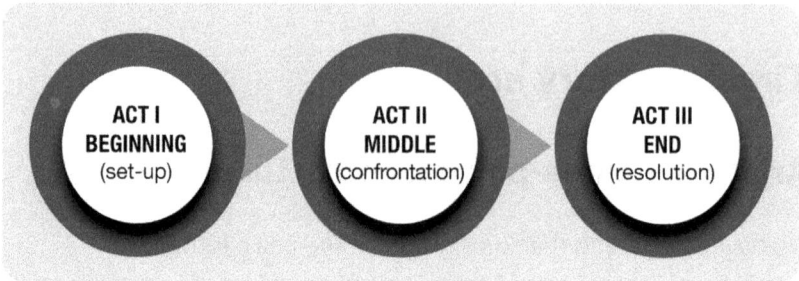

The three-act structure follows this sequence:

Act I: The setup

- This act introduces the protagonists, their world and the central conflict or problem of the story.
- Before the set-up finishes, an incident occurs that disrupts the comfort of the ordinary world and thrusts the main character into action, then the journey begins.

Act II: The confrontation

- This is the longest part of the story and focuses on the protagonist's journey as they experience a series of highs and lows, advances then setbacks.
- There are different points of conflict and many twists and turns.

Act III: The resolution

- This act leads to a climactic confrontation where there is no return for the protagonist – it is a 'do or die' situation, no turning back.
- The conflict is ultimately resolved and the story ends, generally happy ever after.

The hero's journey

The hero's journey, attributed to Joseph Campbell, is built off the three-act structure. The storyline involves a hero who goes on an adventure, faces challenges, learns valuable lessons, wins a victory and, with newfound insights, returns home transformed. Many movies follow this familiar pattern, such as Luke in *Star Wars*, Dorothy in *The Wizard of Oz*, Neo in *The Matrix*, Clarke in *Superman* and Harry in the Harry Potter series.

Here's how the hero's journey follows the three-act structure

- Act I - old world (comfortable world)
- Act II – confrontation / conflict / challenges (all hell breaks loose, meets a mentor)
- Act III – new world (resolution - lessons learnt, becomes a better person, has the elixir to pass on learnings to others).

I lay out the hero's journey framework in the next section on 'Structure'.

Archetypes for leadership storytelling

Swiss psychiatrist Carl Jung's theory of human behaviour is relevant to modern leadership communication. Jung proposed that the psyche is made up of three separate but connected systems:

- **Conscious mind (ego):** what we're aware of, our thoughts, feelings and sense of self.
- **Personal unconscious:** forgotten or repressed memories, feelings and experiences.
- **Collective unconscious:** a deeper layer shared by all humans, containing universal experiences and symbolic archetypes.

The archetypal framework has long been used in the field of marketing. Archetypes represent a brand's personality designed to resonate with the target audience. The idea is that brands identify with an archetype that mirrors the hopes and aspirations of their customers. This means the audience connects instantly with the brand because they see aspects of themselves reflected in the image of the archetype.

The archetypal framework is also valuable in leadership communication because it helps a leader tap into universal patterns of meaning that people resonate with. By aligning with an archetype, a leader takes on a specific language, tone of voice and messaging to evoke the desired feelings and connection within an audience.

Examples:

- The **Hero** archetype inspires courage and action. It is valuable in situations such as starting movements, advocating for change or in times of crisis. For instance, '*Together we can overcome the challenges and shape the desired future we're committed to*'.
- The **Sage** archetype empowers through wisdom. It is valuable in situations where clarity, insight and guidance are needed. For instance, '*Our previous experience combined with the evidence, tells us we're on the right track*'.
- The **Caregiver** archetype is nurturing and emotionally stabilising. It is valuable in situations of high uncertainty where people need reassurance or support to feel safe and secure. For instance, '*We've enhanced our employee assistance*

scheme to 24/7 full access so we can better support staff through this change program'.

- The **Rebel** archetype challenges the status quo by questioning what is and what could be. It is valuable in situations where innovation or new frontiers are desired. For instance, '*The current situation isn't working; let's try some alternative ways to get to where we want to go'.*

The below table shows how some of the common archetypes can show up in different leadership communication approaches.

Archetype	Leadership style	How they communicate	Language/ tone	Promise
The Ruler	Authoritative Takes control Decisive	Big picture Goal oriented Instructive	Bold Opinionated Irreverent	Control
The Rebel	Radical Disruptive Entrepreneurial	Boldness Challenges status quo Direct	Edgy Questioning Challenging	Revolution
The Hero	Bold Action-oriented Takes risks	Courageous Calls to action Leads by example	Confident Motivating	Triumph
The Creator	Visionary Progressive Innovative	Vision casting Blue sky brainstorming Sparks curiosity	Imaginative Expressive Provocative	Originality
The Sage	Intellectual Guide Problem-solver	Imparts wisdom Deep insights Analytical	Logical Reflective Educative	Truth
The Caregiver	Democratic Empathetic Nurturing	Relational Reassuring Empowering	Warm Sensory Inclusive	Safety

When used with volition, a transformational communicator can adjust their communication style and use the archetype most relevant to the context.

For instance, being:

- the **Ruler** during an emergency where people need to follow specific instructions
- the **Creator** when driving innovation in service delivery or product development
- the **Sage** when providing feedback or when planning strategy
- the **Caregiver** when introducing a major organisational change
- the **Rebel** when positioning for market leadership
- the **Hero** when fighting for more resources in a public advocacy campaign.

Types of stories every leader should tell

Leaders need a broad repertoire of story types as well as signature stories in their toolkit, appropriate for different contexts and situations. The types of stories leaders should tell also depends on the intention behind the message, the needs of the audience and the overall outcome to be achieved.

Origin stories

Origin stories are about our roots and build trust by letting our audience know us better. For organisations, they convey information about the founders, why and how it came to be, the problem it solves for customers as well as its values and where it's heading. For leaders, origin stories convey relevant background factors, formative influences, life moments, milestones and experiences that shaped who you are today, your leadership style, your beliefs, values and philosophy.

Personal stories

Personal stories are about a leader sharing lived or worked experiences relevant to a project, process or vision. These stories could be about lessons learnt, past failures and successes or stories of resilience, for example. Leaders who are open to sharing their trials and tribulations, ups and downs, and mistakes and missteps build trust with stakeholders because they demonstrate authenticity and show their humanity. The also creates an environment where people feel safe to try new things.

Purpose stories

Purpose stories are about conveying the 'why'. For instance, why a project or initiative is needed, why a decision was made, why one course of action is better than other alternatives, why now and so on. In change communication, for example, a purpose story would explain the rationale for needing to move away from the past and create a different kind of future. Purpose stories link a project or situation to a worthy cause, thereby establishing a compelling mandate and reasoning for why it makes sense to support it.

Vision stories

Vision stories are about conveying the ultimate outcome or big picture difference a leader wants to achieve in partnership with their stakeholders, followers or community. They paint a vivid picture so people can visualise this desired future. Vision stories can be about a leader, organisation, project, service, program, event or any other leadership initiative. The purpose is to build momentum towards the achievement of the vision by galvanising hearts and minds to act.

Organisational vision statements expressed outwardly (others focused) are more powerful than those expressed inwardly (directed at the company). A company vision that expresses an aspirational future for customers, communities or the planet (outward) will most likely resonate with both employees and customers alike. Whereas a company vision that expresses an aspirational future to be the biggest, best and most profitable (inward) will most likely resonate with management, investors and shareholders only.

That's why outward-focused visions are brand beacons. And inward-focused visions are usually business goals. This is an important distinction for leaders to understand if they're building an employer brand.

Most often, I observe these crucial foundational elements sitting as stand-alone statements on a website or on a poster. As separate statements, they can be dry and not very inspiring, especially if they're not connected or aligned very well. But you can bring these elements to life by weaving them into a compelling origin story or a manifesto as a declaration of what you stand for.

A manifesto is an expression of the core essence of a brand – it makes clear, in a bold and meaningful way, what you stand for and why it matters. It serves as a beacon for your brand, resonating with those who identify with your cause and message – attracting like-minded potential employees and clients.

Brand stories

Brand stories are about conveying value and building trust by letting people know they're in a safe pair of hands. For government organisations for example, brand stories convey value and competence about how they're meeting needs, addressing priorities and solving problems for their customers and communities.

Examples of brand stories are:

- conveying the benefits of different services, programs and events

- explaining policy decisions
- explaining how they're tackling community issues
- giving updates on the progress of infrastructure
- highlighting how they're advocating for resources
- promoting that they're working towards the community vision

Brand stories can also be about thought leadership. For example, about how a leader is championing the way in an area of excellence or innovation. Every team, every discrete service, within an organisation has a brand story that demonstrates value.

Micro stories: small in type, big in impact

Some of the most powerful forms of storytelling are brief, simple and easy to remember. For instance, anecdotes and parables are short stories that are powerful in bringing clarity and conveying meaning. Sharing a personal anecdote can enhance connection between a speaker and an audience. And a timeless parable can encourage people to think deeply about concepts, values and beliefs in a way that data simply cannot.

For transformational communicators, micro stories are versatile tools. They can build rapport with a 'cold' audience, make a message more relatable or understandable in a high-stakes presentation or embed a moral lesson that brings to life organisational cultural beliefs and values for employees.

Below are some examples of how to use anecdotes and parables to inspire deeper connection and understanding.

Anecdote: A brief, real-life story

An anecdote is a short, often personal story drawn from lived or observed experience. The purpose is to illustrate a point, support an argument, impart an insight, convey wisdom, increase emotional resonance or simply to add some humour, interest or entertainment value to a message. Anecdotes are powerful trust builders between a leader and their audience because they humanise the communication process by making the message more relatable.

Examples:

- *'During the pandemic when our main tech system failed, it was a junior member of the IT team who stepped up to save the day with her quick thinking and expert skills. It reminded me that leadership is not about having a title but about service to others.'*
- *'I once worked with a CEO who made time every day to say 'good morning' to everyone with a smile. That changed the culture more than any policy or poster ever could.'*
- *'After running a media skills intensive with a leader, she said, 'Now I finally have words for what I stand for. It reminded me of the transformative power of communication.'*

Anecdotes are ideal for speeches, media interviews, leadership training, team communication or stakeholder presentations.

Parable: a moral or spiritual lesson through story

A parable is a short, simple story designed to teach a valuable lesson, usually related to morality, ethics or spirituality. It often uses relatable characters, familiar situations and straightforward plots to make profound truths accessible. Parables prompt reflection and inspire values-driven, ethical behaviour.

Examples:

- **The lost sheep parable** – A shepherd leaves his flock of 99 sheep to search for one that is lost. He rejoices in finding the lost sheep even though it took time and effort. **Moral:** a good leader goes out of their way to support and guide those lost or in need.

- **The boy and the starfish parable** – A child throws stranded starfish back into the sea one by one. When told it won't make a difference, the child replies, *'It made a difference to that one'* **Moral:** individual actions matter and so do individuals.
- **The two wolves parable** – A grandfather tells his grandson that two wolves battle inside us: one of anger and fear; the other of love and peace. *'Which one wins?* asks the boy. *'The one you feed',* replied the grandfather. **Moral:** we have choice over our mindset and actions.

Parables are powerful lesson givers in keynotes, coaching, mentoring and values-driven storytelling. They help leaders embody wisdom and share enduring lessons in a timeless, memorable way.

Storytelling for influence

Whether our intention is to inform, illuminate or inspire an audience, our message must have persuasive appeal. When crafting your messages and stories, keep in mind the wisdom of Aristotle's three rhetorical appeals for persuasion:

- **Logos** – an appeal to logic, to convince an audience based on reason
- **Pathos** – an appeal to emotions, to convince an audience by evoking feelings, an empathy for the argument
- **Ethos** – an appeal to ethics, to convince an audience of the credibility of the person making the argument.

The logos of your messages captures the logical part of the mind through rationality, grounded reasoning, facts and figures, and evidence.

The pathos of your messages evokes feelings by using specific language storytelling and tonality to trigger specific emotions and feelings.

The ethos of your messages provides evidence of credibility, reliability, trustworthiness, expertise and authority.

When you build logos, pathos and ethos into your leadership messages, you give meaning to the 'why' that sits behind the 'what' and 'how'. The resultant emotional connection becomes a motivational force for employees to fulfill the business purpose and a magnetic pull for those external to the organisation who resonate with your beliefs and values.

Together, ethos, logos and pathos enhance a leader's persuasive influence.

⑦ Reflection questions

- What facts, figures, research and other evidence will appeal to the target audience's logical reasoning?
- What emotions do I want the target audience to feel through my message?
- In what ways can I build trust and credibility with my audience?

Seven pitfalls of leadership storytelling to avoid

Adequate planning and preparation for any communication pays off. It not only increases the likelihood of your message resonating with the audience, it also reduces the chance of being misunderstood or offending someone.

There are many pitfalls to avoid when it comes to leadership storytelling and communication in general. Addressing the wrong audience is up there with the best of them. I'll never forget the time a leader I had prepared a speech for didn't use it. He said he didn't need the speech as he knew what the audience needed to hear and could 'wing it'. In the words of Julie Roberts in the movie, *Pretty Women* – 'Big mistake. Huge!'. As it turned out, he spoke reasonably well, the problem was he thought he was speaking to a different audience! Needless to say, the audience felt disrespected and the leader was embarrassed. It also wasn't good for the reputation of the organisation.

To avoid your storytelling and leadership communication going pear-shaped, here is a list of common pitfalls to avoid:

1. Lack of clarity

One of the most important rules of communication is clarity because a message or story that is vague, confusing or inconsistent will simply land flat or disengage the audience. Lack of clarity is often a sign of inadequate preparation or failing to properly articulate the purpose, intention or desired outcome of the story. Lack of clarity can also be a result of using abstract language instead of concrete language, or the story doesn't hang together well.

2. Failing to tailor your message to the audience

One message, one audience is the rule as a one-size-fits-all communication approach doesn't work. In this overcommunicated world, people only pay attention to what interests or directly impacts them so, if needed, nuance your overarching message or story for different audiences, depending on their needs and preferences.

3. Not making the audience the hero of the story

Stories have a main character and the audience need to see a reflection of themselves in that character for the story to resonate. The leader, as storyteller, is the guide not the hero. The audience is the hero, always.

4. Excessive jargon, acronyms or 'bureaucratic speak'

Using jargon is fine for an audience where it's commonly used, such as using specific words for a group of engineers or lawyers. Bureaucratic language, however, is never ok. Not only because it's formal and 'cold' but because it doesn't sound 'human' and is often confusing. Humanising your communication is one of the best customer service improvements an organisation can make. You'll not only have customers who understand your message, you'll also reduce complaints.

5. Ignoring situational context

Stories, and any other communication for that matter, must be relevant to what's going on in the world of the audience or they won't be of interest. Stories need to answer the 'why now' question and be linked to the broader vision of the company, project or initiative.

6. Over-communication and information overload

Over-communication happens when a leader provides too much information or detail, delivers too many key messages or when the story is too complex. The result is often audience overwhelm, confusion and disengagement. The main message of the story also gets lost so the communication doesn't achieve its desired outcome.

7. Under-communication and lack of transparency

Under-communication happens when a leader provides insufficient information or lack of context so the audience cannot make sense of events. The result is often the same – audience confusion, misunderstanding and disengagement. Insufficient information can be perceived as the leader not being transparent. Being transparent doesn't mean a leader has to convey every detail of a situation; however, it does mean being open and conveying as much information as possible. It also means where you don't know an answer to a question, saying so rather than trying to make up something.

? Reflection questions

- Have I made my audience the hero in my story?
- Which of the archetypes is the most appropriate for my communication?
- What is the best story type to convey my message (purpose, vision, brand)?
- Which metaphor, analogy or parable would make my message more easily understood?
- Am I avoiding the most common pitfalls of leadership communication?

5

Step 4: Structure

*'The structure of a play is always the story
of how the birds came home to roost.'*
Arthur Miller, American actor and writer

Structural models, formats and frameworks in communication give a leader a powerful toolkit for preparing cohesive, aligned and persuasive messages appropriate to the purpose of the communication, audience and specific delivery modality. If words, symbols, images and other inputs are the separate bones of a communication piece, the structural framework is the backbone, providing a strong foundation that gives everything support, enables movement and facilitates the transmission of the message.

There are structures for different situations and settings, such as for media interactions (day-to-day, emergency and crisis), speeches, educational workshops, strategy presentations, stakeholder gatherings, advocacy campaigns, investment pitches, change processes and the like. There are also structures for communication strategies, copy writing, linguistic patterns, persuasive techniques and, as discussed in the last section, storytelling. When it comes to communication, there's a structure for everything.

In this step, we consider a variety of structures for different situations and settings, from messaging and narrative frameworks to presentation formats and media messaging.

Why structure matters

Unstructured communication is fine in the right setting, such as when having a social conversation with someone. But when it comes to leadership communication for purpose, and particularly in high-stakes contexts, structure is a leader's best friend and an 'insurance policy' against mucking things up. Structure is a critical element of communication preparation, development and delivery.

Using structure in communication has many advantages, chief among them providing a way to convey information as clearly and simply as possible. Structure gives order to a list of disconnected thoughts, enables topics to be categorised into themes and creates an outline for the beginning, middle and end of a communication.

With structure, a leader can ensure their ideas are put in the right sequence, with the right timing and the right length. Structure creates order and order clears the mind. Just like having a clean and tidy desk gives a sense of calm and control, so too, structure in communication reduces stress and improves focus.

On the other hand, leaders who deliver their message without structure run the risk of confusing and disengaging their audience because their message lacks clarity, conciseness and cohesion.

Also, there is a difference between structured and scripted communication and both have their place in leadership communication. While structured communication is messaging organised within a framework, scripted communication is a more rigid form where the message is scripted word for word. Media messages, speeches and presentation are often practised word for word; however, the ideal situation is that a leader rehearses their message delivery so that when it's delivered for real, it sounds conversational and not robotic like reading from a script.

Another reason why structure is beneficial is that it helps a leader remember their key points and the order of the points, leaving the leader freer to concentrate on delivering their message with impact.

Strategic communication framework

The purpose of a communication strategy is to provide a framework for the strategic development, alignment and execution of a communication program to support delivery of a leadership project, activity or initiative. Over four decades as a communication professional, I've developed hundreds, if not thousands, of communication strategies; some big, some small, all essential.

While there are many communication strategy frameworks, the framework outlined below provides a holistic end-to-end structure, from purpose through to evaluation. The tables identifies 14 key dimensions of a communication strategy, along with a brief description for each written as quality criteria. This is a handy checklist to use to check each dimension of your communication strategy is correctly formulated.

Communication strategy framework

#	Strategic dimension	Quality criteria
1	Purpose	• The problem/challenge is well defined, and the communication opportunity is clear.
2	Policy	• Relevant policies, procedures and legislation with which the strategy must align are identified.
3	Research	• Research tools and techniques used to understand the problem/challenge are appropriate. • The research provides a foundation to develop strategic objectives and measurable benchmarks.
4	SWOT	• Internal strengths and weaknesses, and opportunities and threats are detailed.
5	Risk	• Economic, social, environmental, political and reputational risks, and their mitigating actions are identified.
6	Objectives	• The objectives are specific, measurable, achievable, realistic and time-bound.
7	Audiences	• Target audiences are defined in terms of their needs, fears, problems/challenges, values and perspectives.
8	Strategy	• The overarching strategic approach is aligned with research findings and objectives, and supports business objectives.

9	Communications	• Vision: the desired outcome is vivid, aspirational and includes a desired future state.
		• Overarching narrative: the foundation narrative explains the 5Ws and H – what, who, why, when, where and how.
		• Key messages:
		  · are brand-aligned, values-driven and include a call to action
		  · include the elements of logos (an appeal to logic such as facts and figures), pathos (an appeal to emotions such as empathy) and ethos (an appeal to ethics such as credibility of the spokesperson)
		  · are consistent across communication channels and customer touch points.

#	Strategic dimension	Quality criteria
10	Mediums	• Mediums are accessible, convenient and preferred by the target audiences.
11	Budget	• The budget is clear and resources are allocated.
12	Implementation	• The execution plan is directly linked to the overarching strategy. • The sequence and timing of tools and tactics are mapped out. • Roles and responsibilities of team members are clear.
13	Results	• The actual results are compared against the measurable objectives. • Logical conclusions are drawn and recommendations for future actions are documented.
14	Measurement and evaluation	• Relevant key performance indicators (KPIs) to measure the success of objectives are identified. • KPIs are regularly monitored and evaluated for accountability and continuous improvement. • All components of the strategy meet acceptable industry standards and codes of practice.

An ongoing commitment to, and application of, quality criteria to your communication strategies will ensure they are of the highest quality.

Three-part messaging frameworks

There are many three-part messaging frameworks because they take advantage of the psychologically-powerful 'rule of 3'. The rule is the idea that people are better able to remember things when in threes. While the frameworks share a similar anatomy, the content differs for each, giving the flexibility to choose a framework best suited to the purpose of the communication and relevant to the topic and setting.

Below is a selection of three-part messaging frameworks, with examples to show how they work.

Classic message triangle

The universal message triangle consists of a simple, three-part structure to ensure clarity:

1. Core message
2. Proof points x 3
3. Call to action

Example:

1. Core message:

'Council is investing $2 million to transform the old public hall into a contemporary and sustainable community hub that will offer a diverse range of opportunities for residents to socialise, learn and get active.'

2. Proof points:

a. *'The old hall is over 100 years old and has reached the end of its useful life.'*

b. *'The old hall doesn't meet the building code or accessibility standards.'*

c. *'There are no other suitable buildings in town to hold large, indoor gatherings. Some residents are becoming disconnected and isolated, and the town is losing its vibrancy.'*

3. Call to action:

'We invite you to participate in the community engagement process to share your thoughts, ideas and ask questions.'

Problem, insight, solution model

This framework applies to crafting messaging related to problem-solving with the insight as the proof point message in the middle. It's particularly useful when addressing challenges or in strategic planning meetings to prioritise different solutions.

Example:

1. **Problem:** *'The old hall is over 100 years old and has reached the end of its useful life.'*
2. **Insight:** *'The local community will support a new community hub being built if they're involved in the decision-making process.'*
3. **Solution:** *'We're going to partner with the user groups and engage the community to help us design the new facility.'*

An alternative to this model when the decision is made is, 'problem, solution, impact'.

Golden Circle model

Renowned leadership author and speaker Simon Sinek's 'Golden Circle' concept describes how inspiring leaders and organisations communicate purpose – their 'why' – to inspire teams. They do this by creating a shared belief about why the organisation exists. This model emphases the importance of starting with 'why' (purpose) before 'how' (process) and 'what' (features). Sinek proposes that when a leader communicates starting with 'why', they inspire action because they are communicating with the limbic part of the brain which controls emotion, behaviour and decision-making. [10]

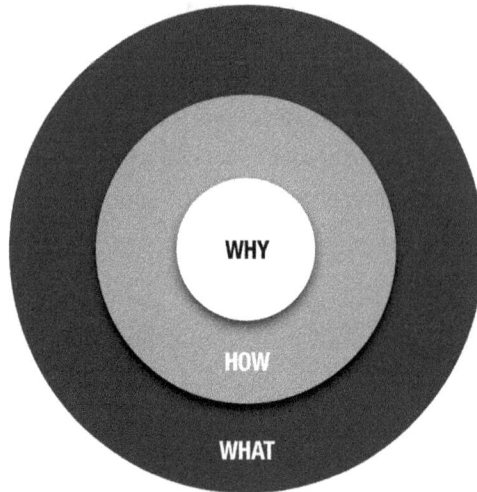

The three-part structure includes purpose (why) before moving to process (how) and product (what).

Example:

1. **Why:** *'We believe all communities should feel a strong sense of belonging.'*
2. **How:** *'We create spaces for people to gather and connect.'*
3. **What:** *'We're building a new contemporary community hub to replace the old public hall that is no longer fit for purpose.'*

Message and strategy house framework

A message or strategy house framework uses the metaphor of a building structure to organise a hierarchy of key messages, with the most important message at the pinnacle, as follows:

1. **The roof** – the core message or overarching theme that captures the throughline of the entire message.

2. **The pillars** – supporting messages that reinforce the core message.

3. **The foundation** – proof points that back up the core message and supporting messages.

Message house example:

1. **Roof (core message):**

   - *'Council has allocated $2 million to transform the old public hall into a contemporary and sustainable community hub.'*

2. **Pillars (proof points):**

   - *'The old hall is not fit for purpose.'*

   - *'It doesn't meet the building code or accessibility standards.'*

   - *'People are becoming disconnected and isolated.'*

3. **Foundation (support messages):**

   - *'Our business case supports a new community hub as the most cost-effective solution and will deliver the best community outcomes.'*

Strategy house example:

1. **Roof (vision):**

   - *'Our vision is to create a welcoming and vibrant central point where the community can come together for connection and celebration.'*

   - *'We're allocating $2 million to transform the old public hall into a contemporary and sustainable community hub for the community to enjoy.'*

2. **Pillars (messages):**

- *'The old public hall is no longer fit for purpose and is costing ratepayers an increasing amount each year to maintain.'*

- *'The old public hall doesn't meet the building code or accessibility standards.'*

- *'People are becoming disconnected and isolated.'*

3. **Foundation (values):**

'This strategic investment by our organisation aligns with our core values of service, respect and empowerment.'

Reflection framework

This framework is a valuable model for analysing experiences, identifying lessons learnt and developing action plans. It guides individuals or teams through three stages: describing what happened (what?), considering the implications (so what?) and deciding next steps (now what?).

Example:

1. **What? (what happened / is happening)** – *'We're investing $2 million to build a contemporary new community hub for the community to enjoy.'*

2. **So what? (why it matters)** – *'The old public hall is no longer fit for purpose and some people are becoming lonely and isolated.'*

3. **Now what? (what's next)** – *'We're inviting the community to participate in a community engagement process to make sure the new hub meets the needs of the community now and into the future.'*

3x3 method

The message matrix is particularly useful when time allows a more extended discussion, such as when giving a presentation to a group of staff or participating in a media interview for a longer article. It can be used in a variety of scenarios and for diverse content. For instance, you can use it to convey the 'what', 'why' and 'how' of something or you can use it to communicate three distinct topic chunks.

To develop a 3x3 message matrix:

1. define **three overarching themes or core messages** to serve as the headlines
2. craft **three support messages** as proof points for each core message / headline.

This gives the leader nine structured talking points to deliver during an extended communication session.

Example: A CEO is addressing employees about a planned organisational restructure.

#	Core message	Support messages
1	'We are entering an exciting new phase of growth for our organisation.'	• Proof 1: 'We've secured 10 new major clients in the last six months.' • Proof 2: 'We've grown market share by 20% in the last two years.' • Proof 3: 'We're planning to go global in the next 12 months.'
2	'As always, our success depends on equipping our people to be the best they can be so they can continue to rise to changes and challenges.'	• Proof 1: 'New leadership training programs start next quarter.' • Proof 2: 'New career development pathways for all staff.' • Proof 3: 'We're strengthening our focus on diversity, inclusion and wellbeing.'

#	Core message	Support messages
3	*'We are committed to making a big picture difference in the world and helping all staff leave a positive legacy through their work.'*	• Proof 1: *'We're expanding our corporate social responsibility program to include sustainability initiatives.'* • Proof 2: *'We're partnering with local environmental community groups to enhance the local environment.'* • Proof 3: *'We're launching an optional new employee volunteer initiative, matching staff with local community groups where they feel they can make a positive difference.'*

Elevator pitch formula

'So, what do you do for a living?' How you answer this question can be a conversation starter or a conversation stopper. Instead of just saying what you do, use the opportunity to also convey who you help and the difference you make for them.

Your job title or profession alone may not be very interesting. But adding the target audience and the impact you make through your leadership role can spark curiosity. Revlon cofounder Charles Revson gave a great impact statement when he once said, *'In the factory we make cosmetics. In the department stores we sell hope'*. This statement inspires me to want to know more.

Example 1:

1. **What I do:** *'I run an audiology practice.*
2. **Who I serve:** *We help people, from three to ninety-three, with a hearing impairment,*
3. **Impact I make:** *to stay connected with loved ones and fully participate in life through the gift of improved hearing.'*

Example 2:

1. **What I do:**   *'I run a recruitment company.*
2. **Who I serve:**   *We help small business owners match the right person to the right role.*
3. **Impact I make:** *This helps them create a positive workplace culture and run a profitable business'*

Example 3:

1. **What I do:**   *'I'm a co-owner of a female-run domestic and commercial painting company.*
2. **Who I serve:**   *We provide tailored paint solutions to properties in the metropolitan area.*
3. **Impact I make:** *We're also an industry trailblazer because we empower women to shake the mould of the typical tradie.'*

Now, I'm both interested and intrigued. Now, you've got a conversation starter.

Narrative structures that move people

Messages on their own can be magnetic but wrapping them in story gives the ability to add context and create more meaning for the audience by taking them on a journey.

Classic narrative structure

This framework, another built off the three-act structure, ties together the past, present and future to help people understand the context, make sense of events and understand where an issue is heading. I use this framework extensively, including for issues management, stakeholder communication, community engagement, and as a basis for change and crisis communication.

The three key elements of this narrative structure are:

1. **Trigger event** - the particular event in the past that created the current situation.
2. **Challenges** - the challenges that now must be addressed in the present.
3. **Goal** - the end outcome the leader aims to achieve in resolving the challenges.

Example: Victorian 2022 flood event

3-Act structure	Timeline	Description	Narrative
Act I (the set up)	Past	**Trigger event** that changes circumstances	'A thriving northern Victorian town was renowned for its friendly locals and iconic tourist attractions. Then, in October 2022, a significant flood event caused devastation across the town, including 90% of homes being inundated.'
Act II (confrontation)	Present	**Challenges to be addressed** because of the trigger event	'The flood caused widespread damage to properties and buildings, and has created significant challenges for the people and economy of the town: • Many residents have had to move out of their home and live in temporary accommodation • Many businesses have closed creating empty shopfronts. • Schools and community organisations couldn't operate for months • Over time, mental health and wellbeing concerns have escalated.'

3-Act structure	Timeline	Description	Narrative
Act III (resolution)	Future	Goal / outcome to be achieved	'All levels of government, in partnership with agencies and the local community, are working hard to address the challenges. A recovery hub has been established, and a range of funding and other supports have been put in place to help the community recover. Funding for mitigation measures are being explored.'

It's important to note that sometimes the trigger event is not readily known, such as when a major technological problem has impacted an organisation, so it may not be possible for a leader to reference a cause or apportion blame. In any event, a leader must always be cautious in apportioning blame unless it is categorically proven or is appropriate given the potential flow-on effects, including legal ramifications.

The hero's journey framework

While there are different versions of the Hero's Journey template, there are typically 17 stages in three parts. If you like the Hero's Journey model for storytelling but find it challenging to create a story that uses all 17 stages, consider using a shorter version of the model, ensuring to maintain the three-part base structure. Below is an alternative version of the Hero's Journey with some key questions to consider when crafting your story.

Part 1 – Old world

- What was work, business or life like before you made the change?
- What was the problem, challenge, frustration, need in your work, business or life that presented itself and had to be resolved?
- Who in your life came along and inspired you to seek the solution to the problem, challenge, frustration or need?
- If there was no particular person or mentor, what was the defining moment when you made the decision to seek a better way of doing things?

Part 2 – The quest

- What fears and challenges – internally and externally – did you face in the journey of seeking to overcome the problem?
- What lessons did you learn along the way?
- What was the ultimate insight, realisation or epiphany you had as a result of confronting the various fears and challenges? Perhaps the insight came to you through a customer experience, a technological discovery, a process improvement, a crisis, a conversation with a mentor or an industry disruption, for example.

Part 3 – New world

- How did the insight change your thinking, beliefs or values, and what was the ultimate transformation for you?
- How are you now using the elixir – the newfound knowledge or insight – to bring value to your clients through your product, service or programs?
- What brand promise do you now deliver to your customers?

When using the hero's journey for narrative, remember that the hero is the audience, not the leader, not the organisation, not the brand.

Pixar story spine

American animation studio Pixar is renowned for its creative and technical excellence in animated children's feature films. It's also well known for its story structure, a six-part framework called, 'The Story Spine'. This structure is an expanded version of the three-act structure and follows a similar story arc to the hero's journey.

The Story Spine framework is as follows:

Act I: Set the scene

1. Once upon a time...
2. Every day...
3. Until one day...

Act II: Confrontation

1. Because of that...
2. Because of that...

Act III: Resolution

1. Until finally...

This framework, not using the exact same wording but same intention, is applicable to business and other settings and scenarios due to its flexibility and simplicity. In some circles, a seventh step is added to the framework – 'and ever since that day...' – to convey lasting impact.

A presentation framework for impact

4MAT model

The 4MAT model was developed by Dr Bernice McCarthy[11] in the late 1970s as a learning framework and instructional design tool that caters to different preferences and styles. It is based on research of four identified learning styles of people, and of right- and left-brain dominance.

It is a useful framework for planning workshops, strategy sessions and other contexts in order to target the broad learning style of:

- people who want to know **why** (people who seek depth and meaning)
- people who want to know **what** (people who seek facts and evidence)
- people who want to know **how** (people who seek practical steps)
- people who want to find out **what if** (people who like contemplating or exploring).

People use both hemispheres of the brain – right and left – but usually have a preference to use one hemisphere over the other. This preference influences the ways people perceive, process and communicate information.

The left hemisphere of the brain seeks to understand through structure and sequence, prefers concrete language to pictures or metaphors and breaks down information into useful bits.

The right hemisphere of the brain seeks patterns, prefers pictures and metaphors to concrete language, and consolidates and synthesises information.

The four points below show how a presentation can be structured to address the four key learning styles and in so doing, answer the why, what, how and what if questions.

1. Why?

The 'why' frame establishes the purpose of the presentation, the environmental context and why the issue, idea or event is important or relevant to the audience, community or humanity. To establish the 'why', use research, stories, benefits, quotes, questions, statistics and the like to create meaning.

2. What?

The 'what' frame tells the audience what they need to know about the issue, idea or event. To establish the 'what', give a definition, tell the history, use relevant facts and figures, case studies and the like to create understanding.

3. How?

The 'how' frame engages the audience to take action, use new skills learned or consider how they can work with you to achieve the desired outcome. To establish the 'how', show the steps to be taken, consider options, brainstorm ideas, use hands-on activities, use hypothetical scenarios, identify tools and tactics, and operational procedures to build skills.

4. What if?

The 'what if' frame engages the audience to consider how thinking or acting may need to be refined, adapted, integrated or reinvented to apply the idea to the external world and into the future. To establish the 'what if', ask the audience to envision the future with the new information learned, give a call to action, suggest a strategy or plan, speculate a new application or refinement, share an insight or key learning to build adaptation.

Frameworks for media messaging

5Ws and H framework

The 5Ws and H framework – otherwise known as the 5WH1 approach or questioning method – is a tool used by journalists to ensure they gather enough information to write a complete story. It's a useful tool for writing media releases and media statements, and to brainstorm the kinds of questions you might be asked in an interview about a particular topic or issue.

Below are examples of some questions.

Consider potential questions	Examples
WHAT questions – establishes the specific act, event or situation	• What happened? • What was the reason / motive? • What does it mean for us? • What will happen now?
WHO questions – identifies the people or groups involved	• Who did it? • Who was impacted? • Who witnessed it? • Who is fixing it?
WHEN questions – establishes time, milestones, deadlines.	• When did it happen? • When did you find out about it? • When will it be fixed? • When can we access it again?
WHERE questions – identifies location, proximity, context.	• Where did it happen? • Where was it found? • Where were they when it happened? • Where are they now?

Consider potential questions	Examples
WHY questions – explains the reason or purpose behind something.	• Why did it happen? • Why now? • Why didn't you know about it sooner? • Why didn't it work?
HOW questions – details the means, mode, method, process.	• How did it happen? • How will you fix it? • How will you prevent it from happening again? • How will you keep us informed?

Media response framework

The universal message triangle, outlined above, is an effective framework to use for crafting a response to a reactive media request. To recap, the three-part structure is:

1. Core message / key point
2. Proof points x 3
3. Call to action

Example, incorporating logos and pathos:

Structure	Messages
Key point	'Council has allocated $2 million to transform the old public hall into a contemporary and sustainable community hub (logos) that will offer a diverse range of opportunities for residents to socialise, learn and get active. (pathos)
Proof point 1	'The old hall is over 100 years old and has reached the end of its useful life.' (logos)
Proof point 2	'The old hall doesn't meet the building code or accessibility standards.'(logos)
Proof point 3	'There are no other suitable buildings in town to hold large, indoor gatherings so groups are booking venues elsewhere.'(logos) 'As a result, some residents are becoming disconnected and isolated, and the town is losing its vibrancy.' (pathos)

Structure	Messages
Call to action	*'We're inviting residents to participate in a community engagement process to ensure this strategic investment by council results in a vibrant, community space where everyone is welcome and feels a strong sense of belonging. To find out how you can get involved, visit our website at …. (pathos)*

From this structure, a self-contained media statement can be developed and given to the media for a news grab or for insertion into an article. By 'self-contained', I mean the statement stands alone; it doesn't need any context around it to make it make sense.

Example of self-contained version:

'Council is investing $2 million to transform the old public hall into a contemporary and sustainable community hub for the community to enjoy. Residents are invited to contribute their ideas and opinions through the community engagement process.'

Frameworks for visual representations

People absorb and understand visual information more quickly and effectively than other modes of communication because visual representations are easier to internalise. Visual models or diagrams are particularly useful for communicating concepts, processes, cycles, relationships, systems or strategies by showing the interrelationships between the various elements.

Research[12] highlighted in a Harvard Business Review magazine (July-August 2025) article found that investors were twice as likely to give a deal the thumbs up when the CEO's presentation was accompanied by a single slide visually illustrating the strategic rationale behind the deal. The research also revealed five key design principles when creating an effective visual representation. These design principles were:

1. **Grouping ideas into three or four main chunks**, such as concepts, pillars or dimensions that together form the base of the model.

2. Within these concepts, **adding layers of detail** to describe the key concepts.

3. **Using colour and shading** to distinguish layers of information.

4. **Indicating clear relationships** among the elements, for instance, with connecting lines or arrows that delineate flows.

5. **Presenting the model in a landscape format** rather than in a portrait format as our horizontal peripheral vision is more expansive than our vertical peripheral vision.

One of the most common models is the three or four-circle Venn diagram. Below is an example of a four-circle Venn diagram showing the relationship between the four key concepts of Ikigai, the Japanese concept that refers to having a sense of purpose in life, a reason to wake up in the morning.

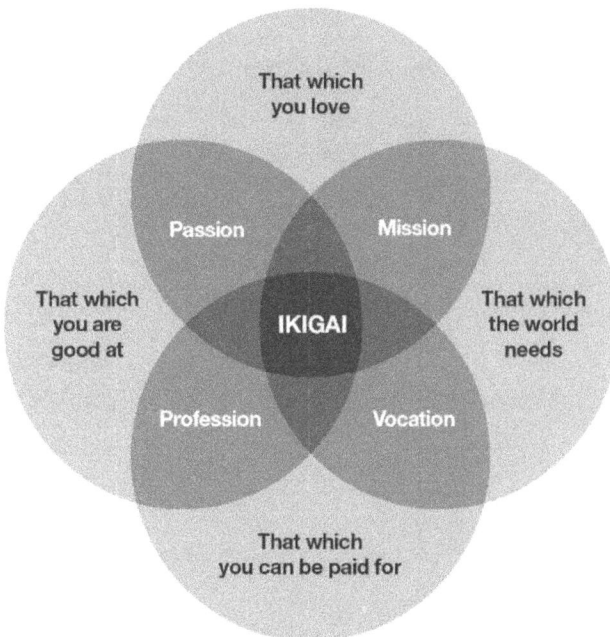

To find the most appropriate model to visually represent your idea, search the internet or the functionality within the documents of your computer or other device.

? Reflection questions

- Does my communication strategy meet all of the quality criteria?
- Which of the three-part messaging frameworks is most suitable for my communication?
- Which of the narrative frameworks will best engage my audience?
- Does my workshop plan cover the four key learning styles of people?
- Have I covered the 5Ws and H in my media interview preparation?
- How can I visually represent my information so it's easier to understand?

6

Step 5: Skills

'Communication works for those who work at it.'

John Powell, classical composer and communication scholar

A message is never just about the words you speak. It is also shaped by how you deliver those words through your voice, tone, pace, facial expressions, gestures and posture. In transformational communication, it's the seamless alignment of verbal language, paralanguage and body language that determines whether your message truly resonates.

For your communication to be influential and inspire action, there must be congruence between your words, your voice and your body language. When these elements are misaligned; when your tone contradicts your words or your body language sends a different signal, for instance, your message loses power and clarity.

Research[13] by psychologist Albert Mehrabian on how people interpret emotions when verbal and non-verbal cues conflict suggested that the impact of a message can be attributed as follows: 7% to the actual words; 38% to the tone of voice; and 55% to body language. While the 7:38:55 ratio is not a universal rule for all communication and applies only where there is emotional incongruence, it does highlight that it's not just *what* you say that is important, it's also *how* you say it.

The good news is that verbal, vocal and physical delivery skills can all be learned and refined. Mastering them builds confidence, enhances presence and dramatically improves the likelihood that your message will land with the meaning and impact you intend.

This step doesn't attempt to turn you into an expert in every aspect of delivery; that would take a book of its own. Instead, I provide some practical insights and simple techniques you can apply immediately to elevate and align your communication.

Verbal language – crafting words for clarity and connection

The power of simplicity

Simplicity in communication is a superpower. Because it's not easy. Simplicity means without complication. Easy means without much effort. Communicating with simplicity takes effort.

- To remove unnecessary words.
- To use short words instead of long ones.
- To use active voice instead of passive voice.
- To use common language rather than jargon.
- To distil complex information down to a single message.

But the rewards are well worth the effort.

- To convey important information accurately.
- To achieve the desired response.
- To create shared meaning.
- To enable collaboration.
- To foster trust.

A little hack you can try when considering how to communicate your next idea, project or initiative, is to summarise it into a single sentence 'log line' or 'through line' that captures the main point clearly and concisely. In movies, a log line describes the central plot. In Ted Talks, a through line describes the central idea. Then test your statement for understandability with a colleague. When you communicate with simplicity, your message is more likely to be understood.

Abstract versus concrete language

Abstract language is that which refers to intangible qualities, ideas and concepts, such as love, vision, trust, beauty, value, health, wellbeing, neighbourhood, community, empathy. Because abstract language is high level and non-specific, it is open to interpretation, which is why it needs to be used in collaboration with concrete language. Abstract language communicates the 'why' of somethings so is best used when wanting to communicate the bigger picture and vision or when a broader perspective is needed.

Abstract language is a key element of transformational communication and research has found that using abstract language can infer power. An article in the *Journal of Personality and Social Psychology* highlights that '*across different contexts and conversational subjects in six experiments, participants perceived respondents as more powerful when they used more abstract language (versus more concrete language)*'.[14]

Concrete language, on the other hand, is that which refers to tangible things, that can be measured or observed, such as a tree, water, building, road or playground. Use concrete words when specificity is needed, such as explaining the 'what' and the 'how' of something. Or when you want to create a more specific picture in the mind.

Here's a quick experiment to demonstrate the power of concrete language. Don't think of a purple elephant. Did the word 'don't' prevent you from thinking of a purple elephant? I'd wager it didn't. Our mind thinks in pictures, not words, and because I said a purple elephant you didn't think of a grey elephant.

Abstract and concrete language are best used with volition and flexibility to serve the purpose of the communication and the needs of the target audience having regard to the context of the situation. During the COVID-19 pandemic for instance, then New Zealand Prime Minster Jacinda Ardern used concrete language effectively to instruct New Zealanders to adapt their behaviour to help minimise the spread of the virus.

Abstract and concrete language are, as movie character Forrest Gump might put it, '*like peas and carrots*' – they go hand in glove. While a bias towards concrete language during times of emergency or crisis is appropriate, communicating shared values around health, wellbeing and teamwork for instance, as well as the bigger picture goal to keep the community safe, makes the communication more complete.

Language patterns that influence

Omne trium perfectum

The Latin phrase '*omne trium perfectum*' means everything that comes in threes is perfect. That's the principle of the 'rule of three' which leverages the brain's natural tendency to find patterns in order to process and recall information more easily. It is based on the idea that three is the optimum number of points to form a pattern of information to make it appealing and aid memory retention.

The rule of three is not only a writing principle, it also extends to storytelling, keynote presentations and visual design.

Some well-known examples of its application are:

- *'Friends, Romans, countrymen.'*
- *'The good, the bad and the ugly.'*
- *'Reduce, reuse and recycle.'*
- *'Body, mind and spirit.'*

- *'Blood, sweat and tears.'*
- *'Three little pigs.'*

Leaders can use the rule of three to simplify their communication, such as focusing on three key messages, three steps, three choices or any other triad combination to make the communication more memorable and impactful for the audience.

Alliteration

Alliteration is the repetition of the same consonant sound at the beginning of words near each other, such as, *'Peter Piper picked a peck of pickled peppers'*. Alliteration gives a rhythmic cadence to words that makes them more engaging, memorable and impactful.

Some ideas to use alliteration are to name a leadership initiative so it sounds more interesting, to give a message a more powerful headline or to make bullet points more memorable. You may have noticed that each of the five dimensions of The Transformational Communicator Method™ starts with the letter 's'.

Alliteration is especially powerful when used with the rule of three, such as 'The most influential leaders communicate with *purpose, power and presence*' or 'Resonant leadership communication is *relevant, relatable and real*'.

Figures of speech

Metaphors, anecdotes and other figures of speech are powerful in providing shortcuts to understanding.

Metaphor: 'This means that'

A metaphor helps explain an idea by making a direct comparison between two unrelated things, stating that one thing is the other and, in so doing, highlighting similarities for emphasis. Metaphors create vivid mental images and make abstract ideas more tangible and memorable. They're powerful for shaping perception, simplifying complexity and inspiring through symbolism.

Examples:

- *'She is a ray of sunshine'*, implies warmth and empathy.
- *'Our organisation is a stoic ship navigating stormy seas'*, evokes resilience.
- *'Our community is a tightly knit fabric'*, conveys unity and belonging.

Some ways metaphor can be used in transformational communication are:

- *'Our purpose is our anchor when times get tough.'*
- *'The community is the lifeblood of the town.'*
- *'Our people are the heartbeat that fuels our mission'.*

Analogy: 'This is like that'

An analogy is a comparison between two different things, often used to explain or clarify a concept. The analogy draws a parallel between the two unrelated things to foster understanding and help audiences grasp relationships, processes or systems.

Examples:

- *'Life is like a box of chocolates; you never know what you're going to get'* – conveys that life is full of surprises; some delight and some don't.
- *'Leading people through disruptive change is like helping someone cross a rickety bridge; they won't go unless they trust*

it will hold' – illustrates the importance of psychological safety and trust.

- *'Cultivating a positive culture is like planting a beautiful tree. It takes time, care and the right environment'* – makes culture more relatable.

Analogies are useful when explaining strategies, values or processes and are especially useful in speeches, presentations and learning environments, such as mentoring sessions or team workshops, to create 'aha' moments.

Message framing for greater impact

Message framing is critical to leadership communication because it conveys a desired meaning or emphasis. The same message, presented in a different frame, can inspire trust or trigger resistance. It can open doors of possibility or close minds before a conversation has even begun.

The frame you choose for a message, including the language and tone, provides the ground upon which to explain, defend or advocate for your idea, decision or project. Framing should not be about spin or leaving out important facts. It should be about the strategic choices leaders make in how they shape, structure and position their words so they resonate with people at a deeper level.

Whether you're managing an issue, introducing a new system or driving change, framing provides a lens of relevance, helping people see why your message matters to them, not just to you.

Six ways to frame your message

Here are some practical ways leaders can frame messages to set an agenda for action:

1. Frame by values

It's difficult to influence people's attitudes and behaviours. That's because when confronted with a new idea, people filter it through their values, beliefs and lived experiences. If the idea fits their worldview, it feels safe and familiar, and the message is more likely to be accepted. On the other hand, if it conflicts, it may be dismissed outright, no matter how logical or well-intentioned it is.

Think about it this way: every audience you communicate with, whether your team, your customers or your community, already has mental models that shape how they interpret the world. Your job as a leader is not to bulldoze through those models but to bridge to them. The frame you choose is that bridge.

Therefore, if you want to influence attitudes or behaviours, frame your idea by attaching it to a pre-existing value or belief of your audience. When you frame with values, you connect to what people hold dear. And by aligning your message to what people already care about, you increase the chance of it landing as intended.

For instance, if you're promoting a new childcare centre, your message could be framed through what matters most to parents, such as children's play, learning, safety and nutrition. As another example, if you're announcing a tight budget to an audience, instead of saying, *'We've created a budget that's frugal but responsible',* reframe with, *'We've created a balanced budget that recognises our responsibility as stewards of our resources and community assets'.* The first message is transactional. The second is relational and principled.

2. Frame by purpose

When you frame by connecting to purpose, you engage hearts and minds around why something matters; something bigger than the task at hand. For instance, instead of saying, *'We're introducing a new tech system'*, reframe with, *'We're introducing a new tech system so we can free up your time for the work that really makes a difference for our customers'*. The focus shifts from process to purpose and people are more likely to engage when they understand the benefits.

Other examples of framing for purpose are in the naming of policies, positions or places. For instance, the 'Speak Up for Safety Program', 'Dads Matter Officer' or 'City Partnerships Grants Program' convey the higher purpose behind the name. In Australia, reframing 'speed cameras' to 'safety cameras' took the focus away from perceived government revenue raising to the higher purpose of creating safer roads. Similarly, the reframing of 'Shark Bay to 'Safety Beach' was an invitation to locals and tourists alike, to come and enjoy the area.

3. Frame with optimism

When you frame with optimism, you energise people by sparking hope and possibility rather than weighing them down with negativity and limitation. For instance, instead of saying, *'That's unlikely to work'*, reframe with, *'Let's give it a go; we have a great opportunity here.'* Optimism sparks momentum while negativity shuts it down. An optimistic frame isn't about ignoring the harsh facts, it's about instilling a sense of hope in spite of them.

4. Frame around vision

When you frame with a future-focus, you show people the path forward and what the future could bring. For instance, instead of saying, *'This change will be a bumpy road for us all'*, reframe with, *'This change will have its challenges but together we can position ourselves for long-term success'.* People are more willing to navigate short-term discomfort when they see a hopeful future on the horizon.

5. Frame around time

When you frame around time, you inject a sense of urgency or plant a seed for the future. If your goal is to influence people's attitudes or behaviours in the short term, then frame the message around a benefit connected to a core need motivational driver that stimulates an emotional response for immediate action.

For instance, instead of saying, '*Due the recent spate of dog attacks in parks, we encourage all residents to have their say on the proposed new Dogs On-Lead Local Law'* reframe to, '*Due to the recent spate of dog attacks in parks, we encourage all residents to have their say on the proposed new Safe Parks, Happy Dogs Local Law so we can put in place some rules that both protect the wider community while also letting responsible pet owners continue to enjoy our open spaces'.* The latter message taps into the motivational drivers of 'safety' and 'love/ belonging' .

Here's another example. Instead of saying, '*We encourage everyone to get involved in a Clean Up Australia Day activity next month'*, reframe to '*We are encouraging everyone to get involved in a Clean Up Australia Day activity next month because every effort, no matter how small, helps create a cleaner neighbourhood and a stronger sense of community pride helps us all keep it that way'.* The latter message taps into the motivational drivers of 'esteem' and 'love/belonging'.

If want to influence people in the longer term, such as create behaviour change around the adoption of a new bin system, frame the message to include the long-term desired benefits while also making the issue relevant to the here and now.

For instance, instead of saying, '*We are changing residents' garbage bins from 120 litre bins down to 80 litre bins in the next 12 months because we need to create a sustainable environment for future generations'* reframe to, *'We recognise that everyone can play a part in creating an environment that's clean and healthy for our families now as well as for future generations. That's why as part of our plans to change residents' garbage bins from 120 litre bins down to 80 litre bins in the next 12 months, we're offering all households a free worm farm so they can make good use of their leftover food scraps while also reducing their waste'.*

6. Frame as 'we'

When you frame as 'we', you create opportunities for collaboration and cocreation of potential solutions. Town hall meetings and stakeholder forums can be a melting pot of viewpoints, emotions and, sometimes, tension. Where there is conflict or many alternative viewpoints, leaders face a choice: defend a position or build a bridge. It's not about winning the argument, it's about creating shared understanding and, if possible, alignment, so you can move forward, together.

Here's three ways to do this well:

- **Acknowledge the concerns**

  Name the concerns you're hearing without sugar-coating or dismissing them. People feel valued when they know they've been truly heard.

- **Connect to shared values**

  Anchor the conversation in the principles everyone can agree on to create common ground strong enough to hold different perspectives.

- **Create space for dialogue**

  Invite diverse perspectives without fear of judgment, then work to connect the dots towards solutions.

When leaders do this, trust grows. Not because one or more groups get their way, but because they believe the process is fair, respectful and transparent.

7. Frame by choice

When you frame around choice, you create agency and opportunities for preferred solutions to be explored or delivered. Framing around choice also enables a leader to explain to stakeholders why a particular decision or course of action was chosen among a selection of possible choices. For instance, instead of saying, '*We are closing the road from 11pm Friday night until 5am Monday morning to complete urgent repair works*', reframe with '*We are closing the road from 11pm on Friday night through to 5am on Monday morning to complete urgent repair works as this option was the most convenient for local residents*'.

8. Frame by blame

When you frame around blame you create understanding through the law of cause and effect. When blame is attributed to a particular person, organisation or other internal or external factor as having been the cause of a particular circumstance, it helps makes sense of events. As a word of caution, leaders need to be careful when using a blame frame as there could be potential flow-on effects, including legal ramifications, depending on the issue.

Framing is a discipline of transformational communication and one which all leaders need to grasp. It elevates your message beyond information only to being both illuminating and inspiring. Because in the end, your choice of words matters. With framing, your audience not only hears your message, but can also feel it, believe it and act on it.

So, before your next leadership conversation, pause and reflect by asking yourself, '*Am I framing this message*:

- *through scarcity or abundance?*

- *through limitation or possibility?*
- *through my lens or through theirs?*

These questions help you check whether your message is being shaped in a way that engages, inspires and aligns, or not.

Avoiding common verbal pitfalls

So far we've talked about tips and techniques to enhance your leadership communication. Here are seven of the more common pitfalls to avoid:

1. Avoid jargon and complex language

Using technical terms or overly complex language where the terms are not common to the audience excludes and disengages people, and makes the leader seem like they haven't understood who they're communicating with.

2. Avoid ambiguity

Vague statements or instructions only serve to confuse an audience, setting up different expectations about what is required. Instead, be clear and concise with language to enhance understanding and for consistent action.

3. Avoid over-communicating

Over-communicating can take many forms but generally refers to talking about something to excess or overloading people with unnecessary information. It can also be over-explaining or over-sharing details when it is not appropriate to do so. Oftentimes, it can involve interrupting or overtalking of others.

4. Avoid under-communicating

Under-communicating, like over-communicating takes many forms but is generally not talking enough about something. It can also be leaving out important details, not being fully transparent, taking too long to get back to someone, or not communicating with them at all.

5. Avoid using filler words

Filler words, such as 'um', 'ah', 'hmm', 'like', 'you know', 'right', disrupt the flow of your speech, are distracting and cause an audience to disengage. Sometimes people don't realise how much they use filler words though some speakers use them to give themselves more time to think – to remember their point or to answer a question. Some filler words like 'well, 'ok' or 'I don't know' are acceptable and conversational.

6. Avoid hedging words

Sometimes called 'qualifying language', hedging words are used to soften or modify a statement to avoid making strong or absolute claims. It can be a single word, such as 'may', 'might', 'possibly', 'anticipate' or it can be a phrase such as 'it appears that' or 'there is evidence to suggest'. It's fine to use this kind of language if you cannot be conclusive or when being definitive is inappropriate, such as when there is a spread of possible answers.

7. Avoid reading from notes or slides

If there's one thing that can diminish a leader's communication impact, it's reading verbatim from notes or bullet points on a slide. It not only makes you look uncertain of your content, it also can come across as mind-numbingly boring. While it's fine to glance at notes from time to time, rehearsing your presentation several times before you deliver it can help you come across with more certainty and sound more conversational.

All these verbal pitfalls detract from your leadership message and diminish your credibility and authority. Avoiding them will help you build trust and connection and come across as the leader you are.

Paralanguage – the voice of influence

Paralanguage includes vocal effects that accompany words such as voice tonality, volume, pitch, pace, pause, even silence. They are crucial elements in oral communication because they significantly impact how a message is received and understood and add to 'entertainment' or 'performance' value of a presentation.

Vocal tonality

I first learned command tonality when I did teacher training many years ago. It involves putting a downward inflection at the end of a statement, so that the tone of voice lowers. It gives the impression you are confident and certain of your content.

Questioning tonality, on the other hand, has an upward inflection at the end of a statement as though a question is being asked. Avoid questioning tonality because it sounds like you're unconfident or uncertain about your message.

Pace and pause

The strategic use of pauses and moments of silence as well as changing the speed of speech, can emphasise key points, allow for audience processing and maintain audience attention.

Energy and vocal expression

Aligning your energy and voice to your message will avoid a mismatch of emotional cues. For instance, when speaking about an exciting initiative or visionary project, being more dynamic with your energy and being expressive with your words will convey more emotion and meaning.

Body language – speaking without words

Body language encompasses facial expressions, eye contact, gestures, posture and personal space, and has a significant impact on the how a message is received. The essential factor? Congruence: your non-verbal signals must align with what you're saying.

When body language aligns with your words and tone, messages resonate deeply; when misaligned, they confuse and undermine trust. By mastering posture, gestures, facial expression and spatial awareness, you harness powerful tools that help ensure your message lands as intended.

Facial expressions that connect

With research[15] showing that people can form first impressions in as little as 100 milliseconds, it's important to be conscious of your facial expressions and the way they could potentially be perceived. Facial expressiveness, including genuinely smiling and steady eye contact, enhances trust and rapport. This is because facial cues carry most of the emotional information in personal interactions.

Gesture with purpose

Deliberate gestures, such as open-palmed hand movements, reinforce what you say and convey a message of trust, that you've got nothing to hide. Slowly nodding shows you're listening attentively and being present to someone.

Posture for performance

Maintaining an upright posture during stressful tasks can improve mood, boost self-esteem, reduce fear and increase feelings of strength and enthusiasm. In one study[16], 74 participants were strapped either upright or slouched during stress tasks. Those sitting tall reported significantly more positive emotions and self-esteem. The researchers concluded that adopting an upright seated posture in times of stress can maintain self-esteem, reduce negative mood and increase positive mood compared to a slumped posture.

The results suggest that leaders would perform better in high stakes situations, which are typically more stressful, if they maintain an upright posture.

Top 10 body language tips

1. Walk in rooms and on stages with purposeful confidence

Before a meeting, interview or presentation, imagine you're walking into a room where people are genuinely pleased to see you. Keep your head up, shoulders back and stride smoothly.

2. Offer a genuine smile to build instant warmth

Offer a soft, authentic smile when greeting someone as you appear more approachable and trustworthy. Practise the 'Duchenne smile (smiling with both your mouth and eyes); it's a warm smile that radiates genuineness.

3. Stand centre stage when delivering key messages

When giving a speech or presentation, physically move to the centre of the room or stage before delivering your main point to anchor its importance.

4. Use open gestures – arms away from your body

Gesture with open arms and with your palms outward rather than crossing your arms or keeping them close to your torso. This signals you have nothing to hide.

5. Maintain an upright but grounded posture

When standing or sitting, keep an upright body with shoulders rolled back, while also staying flexible and grounded. Years ago, my horse-riding instructor drilled this posture into me by telling me to imagine a string attached to the back of my head and this was being gently pulled toward the sky. Similarly, my martial arts instructor taught me to have a stable core and posture by standing feet shoulder-width apart and lowering my centre of gravity through my stomach and hips to ground my position. I still practise both techniques to this day.

6. Face audiences squarely and balanced when answering questions

When answering questions, rotate your body fully toward the person asking a question, ensuring to stand on both feet, rather than resting on one leg which gives the impression of not giving full attention or not caring.

7. Make inclusive eye contact across the room

Ensure everyone in an audience feels they belong by sweeping your gaze slowly to connect with each person, making brief, natural contact. From time to time, making brief eye-to-eye contact with an audience members increases engagement.

8. Blink naturally – avoid fixed stares

Avoid staring someone down by remembering to blink regularly as it makes you look more human and approachable. Adding gentle nodding or a nod here and there shows you're actively listening.

9. Breathe steadily to project calm presence

My riding instructor also used to shout, *'Don't forget to breathe!'*. It's common to hold our breath in times of stress, so bring conscious awareness to your breathing. Pause for a slow, deep breath to steady your nerves and voice. The box-breathing technique is a popular way of slowing down and steadying your breathing so it becomes more rhythmic: inhale quietly for six counts, exhale slowly for six counts, repeat several times.

10. Ensure your words, tone and body are fully aligned

People don't just take in what you say, they take in how you say it. They also watch how you act afterwards. Full verbal and non-verbal alignment is crucial for message clarity and leadership clarity. So, if you say, *'this is an exciting opportunity for our team'* but your tone is flat and your arms are crossed, the message simply won't feel authentic or be believed.

By pairing these tips with regular rehearsal, your non-verbal cues will soon become habitual and unconscious so aligning your verbal and non-verbal communication becomes a natural way of being. This alignment is what makes a communicator not just competent, but transformational, creating trust and connection before a single word is even heard.

? Reflective questions

- Have I included both abstract and concrete language into my message?
- Do I typically have an upward or downward inflection at the end of my sentences?
- How can I incorporate language patterns such as the rule of three into my communication?
- What body language habits do I need to ditch and which ones could I embrace?
- How can I use vocal variety, such as pace and pause, with volition for more effect?
- Is my non-verbal language aligned with the verbal language when I speak?

PART 4

TRANSFORMATIONAL COMMUNICATION IN ACTION

1

Amplifying influence through thought leadership

'The most influential leaders communicate with purpose, power and presence. Because communication isn't just a skill, it's leadership in action.'

Ros Weadman, Transformational Communication Specialist

Transformational communication in action is where leadership truly comes alive. This part of the book brings it all together by providing examples of how to embody transformational communication in different situations and settings. Whether you're amplifying your message as a thought leader, owning the narrative in high-stakes media situations, forging alignment with stakeholders, commanding the room with an unforgettable speech, or motivating teams through change, the way you communicate determines your influence and impact.

However, regardless of the situation or setting, it's important to remember that being a transformational communicator is a mindset, a way of being and doing. The rules of message resonance and receptivity are universal; however, the crafting and delivery of the message is unique to each leader.

Embracing the transformational communication principles of purpose, vision, empathy and grounded reasoning, combined with aligned verbal and non-verbal language, will ensure your words don't just inform but that they influence, inspire and ignite action.

When American singer Beyonce's fans found out she'd lip-synced a performance of the American national anthem on the steps on the White House for President Obama's inauguration, she silenced her critics several days later by opening a press conference with a live rendition of the anthem. She asked all those at the conference to stand up while she belted out *The Star Spangled Banner*, then said, '*Any questions?*' They don't call her Queen B for nothing; it's because she understands the power of positioning.

The professional positioning of a leader can elevate their influence and amplify their message through strategic profile building activities and audience engagement. With the myriad social media platforms and other content publishing opportunities available, leaders can choose where, how and with whom they partner in leveraging their ideas and message in the public domain. This section gives some tips to do just that.

Build your visibility

When it comes to thought leadership, positioning is about distinguishing yourself as a respected authority within a specific niche or industry. Leaders who undertake the strategic process of positioning themselves as thought leaders not only amplify their mission and message, they also build public visibility, enabling their message to reach further afield.

Positioning yourself as a thought leader who shapes conversations and drives meaningful dialogue in your field takes strategy. This is especially true when it comes to selecting the right tools and tactics to deliver your message and connect with the right audiences.

Choose the right mediums

Choosing the right mediums is important to ensure your message reaches your relevant target audience and that you get the best return on your investment. Guessing the right combination of mediums to use to reach your target audience is akin to shooting arrows into the air hoping to hit a target. You could be wasting your time, money and effort if you don't accurately pinpoint your target.

Do some research to find out where your target audience 'hangs out' and how they prefer to consume information. Here are some questions to consider. *What social media platforms do they regularly post on? Do they participate in specific social media forums? Do they read particular newsletters or magazines? Do they attend certain networking meetings or industry events?*

Depending on your goals, you may need to use a variety of mediums. The following list provides a handy summary of mediums that can be used in combination to build your profile, amplify your message and extend your reach.

LinkedIn® profile

I encourage all leaders to establish a personal page on LinkedIn®; it's the social media platform for professionals. It's where jobs are posted, recruiters do their research, industry groups and networks collaborate, and people share their ideas, insights and inspirations.

LinkedIn® is an excellent opportunity to build your profile because at the time of writing, a very low percentage of active LinkedIn® users create content. These are the people who are leveraging their personal brand the most effectively because their content is appearing in the feeds of their connections and followers as often as they commit to publishing it.

When people search your name on the internet, your LinkedIn® profile ranks high in the search results. So, ensure your profile is optimised by using a professional photograph of yourself, a headline that details the problem you solve and for whom, a banner that showcases your key message with a call to action, a featured section that provides clear pathways to work with you and all other sections of the profile completed to the fullest extent.

Publishing content

The creation and sharing of your ideas, opinions and visions in different formats, such as via text posts, videos and articles on social media, or via an e-newsletter to a dedicated database of contacts is a highly effective way of building an audience. You can also share your content by authoring white papers, helpful guides, checklists and quizzes.

Publicity

Publicity is earned media, for example having a news item or opinion piece published in a media outlet, such as a newspaper, magazine, newsletter or broadcast on television, radio or a podcast. Having your ideas, viewpoints and messages carried by third party publications builds authority and credibility.

Visual branding

Creating a visual identity can bring your personal leadership brand to life through such elements as a logo, colour scheme, emblems, symbols and the like. Apply your visual brand elements to every piece of content you create and every touchpoint, including your social media pages, website, newsletters and so on.

Live events

You can hold events to bring together a desired target audience, such as running an online seminar, workshop, breakfast or industry gathering. Or, you can attend others' events, such as networking functions, learning opportunities or conferences.

Lead the conversation

One of the key ways to share your message and viewpoints and increase your visibility is to create a content strategy and ecosystem designed to build your public profile, position you as an authority in your field and increase your newsworthiness for potential free publicity.

This content ecosystem is leveraged off the personal brand foundations you identified and defined in the section of the book on 'Self'. That is, your leadership purpose, vision and values, and your core message, leadership narrative and leadership philosophy.

Writing blog posts and articles, making videos and using technology in other creative ways to share your thought leadership online is one of the most accessible ways to convey your message and build your visibility.

While publishing on relevant social media platforms is a key plank of a visibility strategy, having a central repository of your blogs and articles, such as a personal website or blog platform, is essential so that your wisdom can be found easily and conveniently in one place.

Leverage social media

The social media channels you use to communicate with the target markets you want to influence will depend on where your markets congregate. It's best to choose one or two social media channels and service them well rather than be on four or five channels and service them poorly. Here are some ways to be more engaging and increase engagement on your social media sites.

Have a clear purpose

Begin with the end in mind by asking yourself '*what do I want to achieve by being on this social media platform?*' Each social media platform has its strengths. If you want to connect with other professionals, find new career opportunities or leverage thought leadership among a specific cohort, then LinkedIn® is your go-to platform.

Create quality content

Start by developing a basic content strategy by selecting three key content pillars relevant to your niche or industry category then create content that delivers value to your connections and followers. Content can be informational, educational or inspirational. Personal stories with an insight work well because they are engaging and relatable. Share your original ideas, models and methods. Remember, one post, one message, one audience.

Post regularly and consistently

Posting consistently is more important than frequency. So, choose a realistic posting schedule that you can commit to on your primary social media platform and stick to it. If LinkedIn® is your primary platform, posting two to three times a week keeps you visible. Remember, your posts are not seen by all your connections, only a small portion of them.

Be authentic

Be yourself and write like you talk; conversationally. It's okay to share your highs and lows, successes and failures, as your community will learn and gain valuable insights. If you use artificial intelligence as a strategic tool, edit profusely so it sounds like a 'real' human talking and your own personality shines through.

Comment often

Social media is meant to be, well, social. So, one of the best ways of building trust and connection with like-minded people on social media is to comment on other people's posts. Even if you don't post much yourself, social media algorithms reward those who comment because it adds to the engagement of the platform. Commenting is especially important for leaders, so your connections, followers and others don't just see you as a corporate figurehead but as the caring and thoughtful person you are.

Tell personal stories

People who tell personal stories get good traction, especially if there's an insightful lesson to be shared. Share your wins, milestones and achievements as well as your mistakes, missteps and failures. The key to remember is to share stories that can be helpful in some way to others.

Write for a specific audience

Write with the reader's point of view in mind. This means writing the information in a logical, sequential order, using appropriate language and providing the answers to the questions the reader wants to know. An easy way to assess both order of information and actual content is to write down the top 10 questions you think your target audience might have. You can then organise your points in the order that they might ask them.

Use attention-grabbing headlines

Known as 'hooks' in the social media world, it's important to use a thought-provoking headline to gain attention. Make a bold statement of claim, ask a question, share a fascinating statistic or quirky piece of information. It's also important to close your post with an equally thought-provoking statement that leaves the reader with something to ponder or a next step to explore.

Become a published author

Becoming a published author of a book will elevate your authority status within your industry category better than any other type of publishing. This is because most people recognise that writing a book is a big achievement. Not only because it contains your valuable content – your stories, perspectives, ideas, methods, case studies, models and learnings – but also because writing a book takes dedication and persistence. Even if you don't sell many copies, the fact that you've written a book speaks volumes.

You can use the term 'author' in your bio, on your LinkedIn® profile or in your resume. You can give your book away at workshops, as a Christmas gift to clients, as a door prize or send it to someone you just met at a networking event. You can also use your book to leverage publicity opportunities. The media will often seek out people who have written a book as they are considered subject matter experts who can potentially provide informative commentary for their story.

There are many kinds of books, so the first thing is to be clear on the type of book you want to write. For instance, it could be a book on a specialist area of knowledge, a guide or handbook, or a book of interviews.

A business book is usually somewhere between 25,000 and 60,000 words but can also be much less, depending on the purpose and style. If this seems a lot of words and you don't think you could write that much, you could consider contributing a chapter in book as part of an anthology (a collection of selected writings by various authors). I know many people who have written chapters for books, me included, and they have been wonderful promotional opportunities for their personal brand.

Nowadays, there are many book coaches who can assist you with planning and writing your book, providing feedback on the manuscript and keeping you on track throughout the process. Some coaches can also help you publish and promote your book. There are many publishing options available so it's a good idea to speak with someone who's been there and done that to save you time and effort.

Other publishing opportunities

Here are some other publishing opportunities you can use to build your visibility:

- A website in your name that includes your personal bio, value proposition, certifications, qualifications, awards, showreel and speaking or interview videos, affiliations, publications.
- A regular e-newsletter that includes inspirational and educational content sent to a subscriber list.
- A whitepaper, an in-depth and authoritative report on a specific topic related to your area of expertise that presents a problem and provides a solution.
- Handbooks, guides and templates, which can be useful downloads from your website.

Gain free publicity

If you don't think you've got a book in you, having an article or opinion piece published in a newspaper or magazine, being interviewed on a podcast, radio or television, are also potent ways to build your professional profile.

Publicity is highly effective in building your profile and driving a positive reputation, because it elevates the perception, positioning and profile of your personal brand:

- **Perception** – the credibility and trustworthiness of your personal brand based on what people think and feel. By generously sharing your insights and ideas, you'll build a loyal following over time.
- **Positioning** – the distinguishability of your personal brand compared to others in your niche. By sharing what makes you different, including what you stand for as a brand and the difference you seek to make in the world, you can stand apart from others.
- **Profile** – the awareness and reach of your personal brand in the marketplace. By sharing your message regularly and consistently across platforms, including in the media, you'll become known for the value you bring and the problem you solve.

Publicity can also generate leads for your business, strategic partners or collaborators. Most people are walking around in a state of 'latent purchase readiness' just waiting for the right moment to buy something. They may have done their research but not yet made up their mind. Seeing your published article or listening to your podcast interview just might help them take that next step.

Types of media

Media can be segmented by owned, bought and earned **content**:

1. **Owned media** – content you create, such as your website, blog, social media posts, brochure newsletter, LinkedIn® profile, webinars, media releases, articles, opinion pieces, podcasts (yours).
2. **Bought media** – content you buy, such as display ads, advertorials, pay per click, boosted content, retargeting, sponsorships, trade shows, paid influencers.
3. **Earned media** – content about you that you didn't create or pay for, such as testimonials, reviews, social likes and shares, brand mentions, media coverage such as published articles and editorial, podcasts (others).

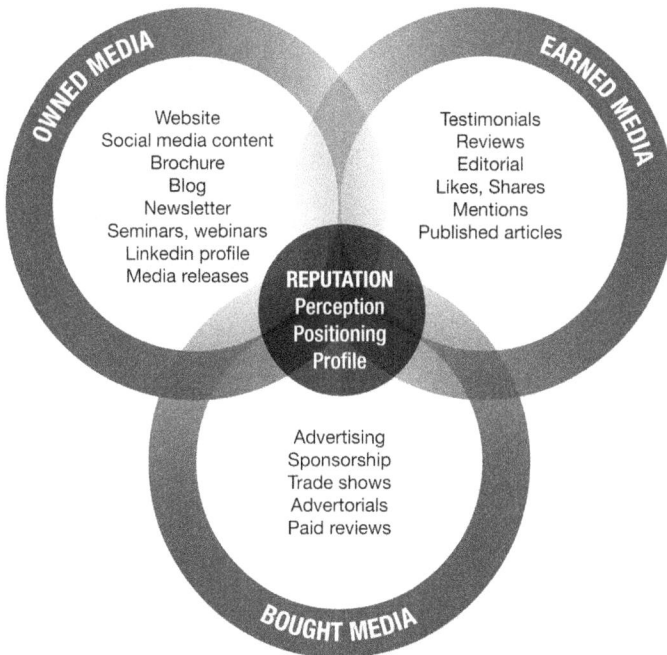

Owned, bought and earned media model

225

Publicity, in the form of a published article or podcast interview for example, is also earned media. Publicity, as earned media, is more powerful than owned media (a blog) or bought media (a paid ad).

This is because publicity content about you created or carried by a third party is more credible because it doesn't seem like self-promotion. That's why testimonials – as earned content – are used by businesses; because someone singing your praises is more believable than you doing it yourself.

Media can be segmented by **format**:

- **print media**, such as newspapers, magazines and journals
- **broadcast media**, such as radio and television
- **digital media**, such as podcasts, enewsletters and emagazines.

Media can also be segmented by **audience**:

- **specific industries** or **topics** for targeted audiences
- **geographic audiences**, such as local, regional, state, national or international mediums for mass audiences.

Using the media to increase your visibility is only effective when you target the right media with the right message for the right audience at the right time.

? Reflection questions

- Is my LinkedIn® profile optimised?
- What social media platforms could I be active on?
- How could I leverage my core leadership message and philosophy to lead the conversation in my niche?
- What three content pillars could form the basis of my social media content strategy?
- What industry conferences could I speak at, within my niche, industry and beyond?
- What media outlets, magazines and newsletters could carry my opinion piece?
- What would be a good title for a book I could write?

2

Owning the narrative in high-stakes media interactions

'In the age of information, credibility is your currency.'
Ann Curry, award-winning journalist

Three universal truths

What I've come to know in my four-decade-plus-long career as a communication professional, is that even the most experienced media spokespeople can come unstuck. Becoming a confident and competent media spokesperson is critical for leaders because there's a lot at stake. Not just your personal reputation. But the words you say in public and in the media can also impact the organisation you represent and, sometimes, third parties.

We've all seen media interviews go well and we've all seen them go pear-shaped. I'll never forget the day at the height of a crisis, the leader spokesperson on the issue, who had performed brilliantly under the extreme pressure of daily media conferences and community outrage for days on-end, got burned by the media.

Unbeknown to the leader, the camera was rolling in the preamble chat with a journalist prior to a prerecorded television interview. The journalist asked a difficult question and in that the moment, the leader had closed body language, a screwed up facial expression and couldn't quite get the right words out. As it happened, it was the preamble chat footage that made it on the television news that evening. Suffice to say, the leader was heavily criticised by the public for a perceived lack of empathy and it didn't help the organisation's position in managing the crisis.

In another television encounter that didn't end well, the CEO of a large corporation was heavily criticised for walking out halfway through a pre-recorded television interview. The CEO made a statement they immediately regretted and wanted the journalist to retract the statement but the journalist determined that all statements were on the record and would not remove the 'offending' footage. Again, that became the viral news story rather than any other part of the interview.

The fatal mistake of both leaders was to presume that there's such a thing as 'off the record'. In my experience and as demonstrated in these two examples, 'off the record' is discretionary, and certainly not in the control of the spokesperson. It is these types of experiences that have led me to believe there are (at least) three universal truths when it comes to media interviews:

1. It's not what happens but how you handle it that matters.
2. It's not just what you say, it's also how you say it.
3. The only thing you can control is yourself.

That's why preparation is key! Because when there's proper preparation for every media interaction, then there's an optimised opportunity for a leader to get their message across confidently, competently and with an increased likelihood of it landing as intended.

Understanding the media

Like any relationship, media relations is about nurturing positive relationships, meeting needs and expectations, and establishing a mutually-beneficial value exchange. Inhouse communication teams work hard to build and maintain positive working relationships with journalists and optimise the value exchange process for the organisation.

In the case of publicity, the value exchange is your newsworthy content (story idea/words, interview, images, video) for potential published space or airtime and access to an audience.

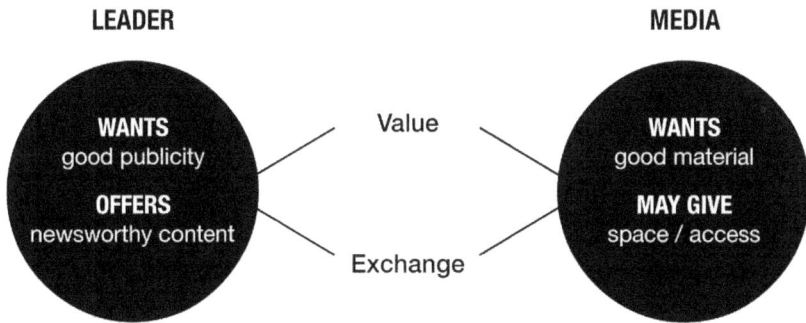

LEADER　　　　　　　　　　　　**MEDIA**

WANTS good publicity

OFFERS newsworthy content

Value

Exchange

WANTS good material

MAY GIVE space / access

Media value exchange process

While there are no guarantees when it comes to publicity, understanding the media and satisfying its needs can vastly increase your chances of a successful media interaction.

Types of media interactions

There are two types of media interactions: questions in and questions out.

Questions in is when the journalist's questions *do* appear in the final version of the story. This is where the audience can see, hear or read both the interviewer questions and the interviewee responses, such as in live interviews on radio or television, talk back programs, longer articles published as an interview and in podcasts.

Questions out is when the journalist's questions *do not* appear in the final version. For example, when a news grab is provided for on-the-hour or nightly news bulletins, general stories, or TV programs where edited comments are used.

When agreeing to participate in a media interaction – and you do have a choice – it's important to know whether the questions will be in or out as each format requires a different approach to preparing for the media interaction. For example, a media interaction that will result in the interviewer's questions being included in the final story will require substantially more preparation and an arsenal of key messages and proof points than if the story includes a stand-alone quote, such as a short news bulletin.

10 criteria for assessing newsworthiness

The media uses certain criteria to determine the newsworthiness of a story. In other words, how likely the story will be of interest and relevance to their audience. When being proactive with your media program, you can use the same criteria to determine the likelihood of your story getting a run in the media.

Here are 10 criteria to assess the newsworthy value of a story:

1. **Impact** – the degree of impact on people, the community, the world
2. **Relevance** – whether the topic is on trend or important in the context of life right now
3. **Appeal** – the level of interest the story is likely to have with a specific audience or the wider public
4. **Conflict** – as with the three-act story structure, a story needs an element of confrontation or at least two opposing sides or contrary viewpoints
5. **Proximity** – how local the story is, the more local, the more relevance to the audience
6. **Prominence** – whether the subject of the story is iconic or has celebrity status
7. **Timeliness** – the timeframe of the topic, whether in the immediate-, short- or long-term
8. **Quality of 'talent'** – the relevance, authority, authenticity and 'entertainment' value of the spokesperson, including their ability to deliver interesting and engaging quotations
9. **Quality of materials** – sources of information are verifiable, audio and visual content is interesting and high quality
10. **Entertainment value** – the degree to which the story will engage an audience and keep their attention

When you understand the criteria to assess newsworthiness, you better understand what makes the media tick and how you can be successful in your media interactions.

Preparing for day-to-day media interactions

All media interactions, whether responding to a day-to-day general enquiry or providing a holding statement in times of emergency or crisis, require adequate preparation. To simply 'wing it' is a high-risk approach that I strongly advise against. It reduces the potential of your message coming across as intended and may compromise your professional credibility and strategic positioning on the topic.

The three-step **'Clarify, AIM, Deliver'** preparation process will stand you in good stead for handling media interactions in all situations. What follows is an explanation of the process along with examples of each phase.

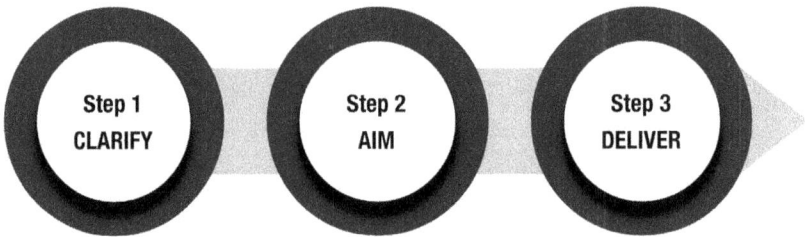

Clarify, AIM, Deliver media preparation process

Step 1: Clarify

When contacted by the media, ask a series of clarifying questions to help you determine whether or not you wish to participate in the opportunity. The table gives a guide to the types of questions to ask a journalist.

Clarify	Considerations
Media outlet	• If the journalist says they're from the ABC, ask if it's ABC radio or television, regional, metropolitan or national. • Also ask if the media opportunity is for a news bulletin, a live interview for a program or a longer article, for example. This will help you determine if questions are out or in.

Clarify	Considerations
Nature of request	• What is the topic or issue? (Assess this topic against the newsworthy criteria as this gives insights into the significance of the issue and potential coverage) • Will they provide the questions in advance? If not, ask their general line of questioning or what they specifically want a response to.
Deadline	• What is their deadline to receive your response?
Date of publishing	• When will the story be published / broadcast?
Other spokespeople	• Who else are they speaking to?
Mode of delivery	• What is their preferred way of receiving a response? • interview over the phone / in person / via video conference? • written response? • audio grab? • video footage?

As part of the preparation process, I also advise leaders to consult with their inhouse media and public relations team to consider four key elements:

1. **Enquiry status** – has the organisation received a similar enquiry from another media outlet. If yes, has the organisation already responded?
2. **Participation** – is it beneficial and appropriate for the leader to participate in the media opportunity and will it serve their audiences?
3. **Spokesperson** – who is the most appropriate spokesperson based on the topic and its significance?

Sometimes it's appropriate to have two spokespeople. For instance, in one crisis situation I managed where there was highly technical information to convey, at press conferences we used the leader of the organisation to deliver the key community messages and a subject matter expert to answer questions of a technical nature.

4. **Questions** – what are the likely questions to be asked by the journalist? Use the 5WH1 question method (what, who, when, where, why and how) outlined in the section on 'Structure' to consider the types of questions you might be asked in a media interview.

You're now ready to AIM your message.

Step 2: AIM

The AIM media messaging framework covers three key considerations:

1. **Audience** – who you want to speak to
2. **Intention** – what you want to achieve
3. **Message** – what you want to say

A message isn't just what you want to say; it's how it's received that matters. If your message doesn't resonate with the target audience, then it is a wasted opportunity to get your message across, and advance your goals and priorities. That's why analysing the target audience before crafting the message is crucial.

1. Audience – who you want to speak to

Analysing the audience first is crucial because it means you can craft a message that is more likely to resonate with them. We covered how to analyse audiences in detail in the section on 'Stakeholders' so I'll simply recap here.

To understand your audience consider these three elements:

- **Target audiences** – the primary audience is the main target for the media message because they are directly affected by a decision, event or situation. The secondary audience is a not directly impacted but they still hold some level of interest or impact.
- **Psychographics** – the attitudes, beliefs, values, expectations fears and aspirations of the target audiences.
- **Core needs** – as identified in Maslow's Hierarchy of Needs.

You should also consider the audience's language preferences, and what they know and don't know about the topic in question.

2. Intention – what you want to achieve

Once there is a clear understanding of the audience, then crystallise what it is you want to achieve from the media opportunity.

To clarify your intention consider these three elements:

- **Goal** – what is the communication goal you want to achieve through the media interaction? For instance, do you want to:
  - **inform** people to raise awareness?
  - **invite** people to get involved?
  - **educate** people to increase understanding?
  - **persuade** people to take action?
  - **recognise** peoples' achievements?

- ◦ **inspire** people to unite in pursuit of a worthy goal?

- **Emotion** – how do you want people to feel as a result of hearing your message? For instance, do you want them to feel:
  - ◦ happy?
  - ◦ disgusted?
  - ◦ surprised?
  - ◦ angry?
  - ◦ proud?
  - ◦ inspired?

- **Action** – what do you want the audience to do as a result of your message? For instance, do you want them to think differently or take action? If, so, give your message a **call to action** so the audience knows the next step to take. For example:
  - ◦ have your say
  - ◦ sign the petition
  - ◦ attend this event
  - ◦ consider this option
  - ◦ participate in the engagement process
  - ◦ go to our website for more information
  - ◦ stay away from the area until the emergency services give the all-clear.

3. Message – what you want to say

Before crafting your message, revisit part 1 of this book which outlines the key insights of a great message. Below I've included seven key criteria to keep in mind:

1. **Conviction** - Conviction to your message is the most important because it conveys belief, confidence and authority.
2. **Simplicity** - The simpler the message, the easier it is to say and remember.
3. **Positioning** - A message needs to have a distinct position in relation to an issue for it to carry weight.
4. **Repetition** - Reinforce the key message often.
5. **Relatability** - The message taps into the fears, frustrations and hopes of the audience and uses common language.
6. **Persuasive** - The message contains logical reasoning and evokes feelings, and the spokesperson is credible.
7. **Aligned** - Your language, voice tonality, body language and actions must match the message.

Over the page is an example template to use to craft your media messages

AIM media message template

Use this template as a guide to prepare for a media interaction.

Media outlet:	Journalist:		Date:	
Topic:				
Newsworthy values:				
AUDIENCE	Primary		Secondary	
	Motivational driver		Motivational driver	
INTENTION	Goal		Goal	
	Emotion		Emotion	
	Action		Action	
MESSAGE Long version	**Key message 1** Key point: Proof point 1: Proof point 2: Proof point 3: Key outcome:		**Key message 2** Key point: Proof point 1: Proof point 2: Proof point 3: Key outcome:	
Short version (For news grabs)	**Self-contained version**		**Self-contained version**	

Example:

The below example brings the three parts of the media message together and provides a short, self-contained version for a media grab.

1. **Key point**

   'Council has allocated $2 million to transform the old public hall into a contemporary and sustainable community hub (logos) that will offer a diverse range of opportunities for residents to socialise, learn and get active.' (pathos)

2. **Proof points**

   a. *'The old hall is over 100 years old and has reached the end of its useful life.' (logos)*

   b. *'The old hall doesn't meet the building code or accessibility standards.' (logos)*

   c. *'There are no other suitable buildings in town to hold large, indoor gatherings so groups are booking venues elsewhere. (logos) As a result, some residents are becoming disconnected and isolated, and the town is losing its vibrancy.' (pathos)*

3. **Key outcome**

   'This strategic investment by council will provide a much-needed, multi-use facility for the community, and a future-proofed council asset. (logos) It will be a vibrant community space where everyone is welcome and feels a strong sense of belonging.' (pathos)

Self-contained version

'Council is investing $2 million to transform the old public hall into a contemporary and sustainable community hub that will provide a diverse range of programs and multi-use spaces. The new facility will be a vibrant community focal point; a welcoming place where everyone belongs.'

Step 3: DELIVER

This step is all about how a leader performs in a media interaction, which is a combination of verbal and non-verbal communication. Below are some interview tips and general advice to keep in mind for media interactions. I also encourage you to refamiliarise yourself with the 'Skills' section of the book.

Staying in control

The following tips will help you stay in control of an interview:

- **Don't let a journalist put words into your mouth**. If a journalist says, *'So, what you're saying is...'* or *'Do you mean...?',* for clarity and consistency across the media, it's best to respond in your own words by repeating your key message.
- **Stop interruptions**. Address interruptions from the outset with statements such as, *'Please let me finish...'* or *'I'll just finish my point...'* or *'I'll respond to that in a moment. I'd first like to say...'.*
- **Respond to the journalist's statements as well as questions**. A lack of addressing a point made may come across as agreement or appear like the interviewee is avoiding the issue.
- **Don't respond to a question you don't understand**. Ask the journalist to repeat the question or paraphrase it back for clarity, such as, *'Do you mean...'* or *'Are you asking...'.*

- **Stay on track**. Avoid an interview going off topic by using a bridging phrase to bridge back to the main topic and your key message.

- **Don't answer a question you don't know the answer to**. If you don't know the answer to a question, say so and commit to getting back to the interviewer. For instance, '*I don't have that information at hand; however, I'll find out and get back to you...*'.

- **Stay calm and rational**. If an interview turns hostile, continue to respond calmly, directly and succinctly with aligned message, voice and body language.

Communicating in emergency and crisis situations

Being a spokesperson in an emergency or crisis is different to day-to-day situations in many ways because of the heightened stakes.

- The timeframe is urgent.
- The environment is more frantic.
- The media are more frenzied.
- The situation unfolds unpredictably.
- The potential impact on people is more significant.
- People are likely to be confused.
- Information is incomplete.
- Bad news travels like wildfire.
- The potential for reputational risk is higher.

Because of these factors, leaders must rehearse different scenarios as part of a formal crisis communication plan so they are as prepared as possible for such events before they happen.

The difference between emergency and crisis communication

In most cases, emergency communication relates to an external incident, such as a major traffic accident, gas leak, crime, fire, flood or natural disaster caused by extreme weather. In emergency situations, a third party (such as the State Emergency Service, police, fire authority or relevant government department) is the lead agency.

Crisis communication, on the other hand, relates mostly to an internal incident or matter that heightens reputational risk, such as operational meltdowns, product recalls, workplace accidents, misconduct of individuals, cyber-attack or other business disruption event. In an internal crisis, the organisation is the lead agency.

This delineation between emergency and crisis communication is important for the purpose of clarifying which agency takes the lead in communicating the situation; but there is no doubt an emergency can escalate into a crisis when there is a threat to life. Also, an organisational crisis might not have a threat to life.

Leaders are judged on how they handle an emergency or crisis

How a leader manages an emergency or crisis can either enhance or diminish their reputation based on how the public views their performance. Things rarely go well for a leader who ghosts the public or goes missing in action when people feel they are needed most. On the other hand, the public's trust in, and respect for, a leader can grow when they step up to the plate and lead through open and empathetic communication.

Leaders who fell on their sword

In 2019, then Australian Prime Minister Scott Morrison was holidaying in Hawaii when major bushfires were burning out of control in New South Wales. Deciding not to come straight back to Australia and remain on vacation was not well received by the Australian public. Although he did eventually cut his holiday short and returned to address the unfolding tragedy, the reputational damage was done. In addressing the public sentiment at a press conference, Mr Morrison conceded he caused *'great anxiety in Australia'* and with the benefit of hindsight he would have made a different decision.[1]

Former Victorian Police Chief Commissioner Ms Christine Nixon also experienced the wrath of the public when, during the Black Saturday bushfires of 2009 in which 173 people lost their lives, she chose to go out for dinner as the fires raged. It was later reported that in an open letter published in several Melbourne newspapers, Ms Nixon apologised for her actions stating, *'I understand that some of my decisions on that day have upset some people, in particular my leaving the control centre in the evening, and for this I apologise. In hindsight, would I have done some things differently on that day? Yes I would.'*[2]

Leaders who rose to the occasion

Anna Bligh served as the 37th Premier of Queensland, from 2007-2012, and was the state's first female Premier. She earned high praise for her communication skills in rallying the people of Queensland during the devastating 2010-11 floods.

Bligh's *'We are Queenslanders'* speech, delivered at a press conference on 12 January 2011, was one of the most inspiring I've heard by a public official during an emergency. Below is a poignant excerpt.

> *'...as we weep for what we have lost, and as we grieve for family and friends, and we confront the challenge that is before us, I want us to remember who we are.*

*We are Queenslanders; we're the people that they breed tough north
of the border. We're the ones that they knock down and we get up
again. I said earlier this week that this weather may break our hearts
and it is doing that but it will not break our will and in the coming
weeks and in the coming months we are going to prove that beyond
any doubt. Together, we can pull through this and that's what I'm
determined to do and with your help, we can achieve that.*[3]

Findings of a study on the perceived styles of leadership of
Queensland Premier Anna Bligh and former Australian Prime Minister
Julia Gillard during the Queensland floods showed Bligh to be
inspirational and charismatic, and Gillard's communication style to be
'robotic and rehearsed'.[4]

An analysis of Twitter posts that mentioned the two leaders show that
posts about the leadership style of Bligh were consistently positive,
with praise for her charisma, inspiration, intellectual stimulation and
individualised consideration. de Bussy and Paterson[74] found that
politicians who display charisma and leadership during a disaster are
viewed by their publics to be effective political leaders. Those who
display such traits are seen as expressing concern for individuals
affected by the disaster while also showing strong political leadership.

As mentioned earlier, New Zealand Prime Minster Jacinda Ardern was
highly praised for her communication during the COVID-19 pandemic,
giving clear instructions on how New Zealanders could adapt their
behaviour to help minimise the spread of the virus.

An article in Rutgers Business Review points to many studies that
highlight the successful communication of female leaders during the
COVID-19 crisis in guiding action and promoting compliance. The
article says that, *'research shows that states led by female governors
in the United States saw fewer coronavirus-related hospitalizations
and fewer deaths than states led by male governors. Similarly, cross
country comparison data demonstrates that even after controlling for*

socio-economic disparities, female leadership resulted in overall lower levels of coronavirus transmissions and deaths'.[5]

Holding statement frameworks

The frameworks below provide a guide to drafting initial holding statements during an emergency or crisis. These frameworks should be considered as a guide only and adapted as appropriate, based on professional advice from public relations, governance, risk and legal practitioners, depending on the issue and the specific situation.

Media holding statement structure – emergencies

Point	Criteria	Description
1	**What happened**	Reiterate known facts as identified and conveyed by the lead agency.
2	**Who was impacted**	Reiterate known facts about those impacted, if appropriate. No names.
3	**How it is being addressed**	Explain how the organisation is supporting the lead agency and helping those impacted.
4	**Communication updates**	Commit to further updates.
5	**Call to action**	Provide instructions so people can take action to stay safe.

Media holding statement structure - crisis

Point	Criteria	Description
1	**Acknowledgement**	Acknowledge the situation and provide information that can be made public.
2	**Challenges**	Identify challenges being addressed.

Point	Criteria	Description
3	**Reassurance**	Reassure people and give confidence that all that can be done is being done.
4	**Goal**	Say what outcome the organisation is working towards.
5	**Empathy**	Express empathy to those impacted. Apologise as appropriate.
6	**Gratitude**	Thank all those helping and all those waiting.
7	**Communication**	Commit to regular updates.
8	**Call to action**	Provide direction to those impacted so they can take action.

In any emergency or crisis, there's no doubt the best approach is to get on the front foot by being proactive. Because when there is no leadership communication an information vacuum occurs, leaving it open for people to fill with their own judgements and assumptions. Be an open communicator in good times and bad, and you'll earn the trust and respect of your employees and other stakeholders.

(?) Reflection questions

- Have I analysed the audience's psychographics and do I understand their attitudes, beliefs fears, expectations and aspirations?
- Have I considered the audience's common language and what they know and don't know?
- Have I clarified my intentions:
  - goal to be achieved?
  - emotion to evoke?
  - desired audience action?
- Does my message answer the 5Ws and H?
- Does my message include logos (logical reasoning) and pathos (emotional resonance)?
- Are my leadership voice, beliefs and values woven through my message?
- Does my message align with the principles of a great message?
- Am I setting aside time to rehearse my key messages and practise answering questions in a mock interview?

3

Building trust and alignment with stakeholders

'Trust is the glue of life. It's the most essential ingredient in effective communication.'

Stephen R Covey, author of The 7 Habits of Highly Effective People

A primary way leaders forge strong relationships with stakeholders is through transparent, purposeful communication that seeks to build common ground and align diverse interests. This is the essence of transformational communication. This section of the book gives guidance on how to effectively manage stakeholder relationships, whether embarking on a community engagement process, leading a townhall meeting, conducting a strategy session or driving organisational change. It focuses on establishing open communication lines, fostering understanding and create positive change, together.

Engaging stakeholders for better decision-making

Government organisations make thousands of decisions that impact peoples' lives. From the delivery of myriad human services to large scale infrastructure projects and everything in-between, the suitability and acceptance of these decisions largely depends on how well governments engage with those stakeholders who will be affected by the decisions.

While not everyone affected will agree with the decision, if a government authority has conducted a transparent, genuine and robust community engagement process in making the decision, acceptance and support is more likely.

Conversely, as stated in the VAGO *Public Participation in Government Decision-making – better practice guide*: *'Failing to adequately engage the public risks alienating the community and creating negative impacts through poorly informed and implemented decisions'.*[6]

While most government organisations have a corporate communications strategy and a separate community engagement framework, I have found a combined strategic communications and engagement approach to stakeholder relations is the most effective way of ensuring two-way dialogue, paving the way for building trust and achieving mutually-beneficial outcomes.

An integrated strategic communications and engagement approach can help organisations avoid the following stakeholder relations pitfalls:

- not closing the loop with stakeholders
- using the incorrect level of engagement
- lack of alignment with strategic plans
- not engaging all relevant stakeholders
- perceived lack of transparency and accountability by the community
- ad hoc engagement communications
- stakeholders not fully understanding their rights or the ramifications of a government decision.

Blueprint for transformational stakeholder engagement

I developed the **Core Communication Method for Stakeholder Engagement™** methodology to underpin my work and training with government organisations. The method combines strategic communication and community engagement approaches to help government organisations deliver the right messages to the right stakeholders through the right mediums, and engage them at the right level, using the right techniques at the right time.

I have reproduced the key elements of the methodology here as they apply not only to government community engagement processes but can be adapted to other forms of stakeholder management, such as customer relations or investor relations.

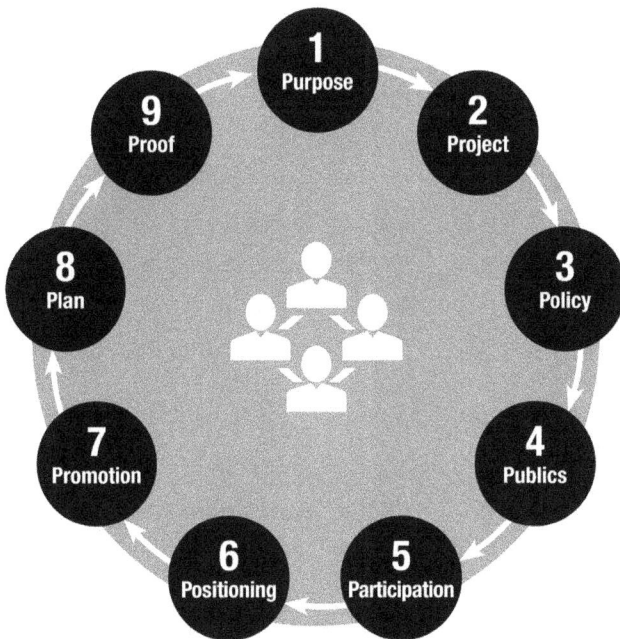

Core Communication Method for Stakeholder Engagement™
©Ros Weadman

The key elements of the nine dimensions of the **Core Communication Method for Stakeholder Engagement™** method are summarised below.

Step 1: Purpose

Outlines why the engagement process is needed, the communication opportunity to be leveraged and expected key outcomes.

Step 2: Project

Outlines why the project is needed, a SWOT (strengths, weaknesses, opportunities and threats) analysis, a risk/issues profile with mitigation measures, and strategic communication goals and objectives.

Step 3: Policy

Outlines the policy and the legislative and strategic context to understand key drivers for the project and ensure alignment with internal policies, plans and strategies.

Step 4: Publics

Identifies and analyses internal and external stakeholders to understand the different levels of interest and powers of influence in relation to the project, and their communication and engagement needs.

Step 5: Positioning

Outlines the overarching strategy for positioning the project within the current and future community context. This section also includes positioning communications, such as:

- project vision
- value proposition
- master narrative

- supporting key messages for FAQs
- responses to key objections.

Step 6: Participation

Outlines the engagement approach, the question to be explored and recommended engagement techniques and activities, to capture the views and ideas of stakeholders. This also includes closing the loop on all engagement processes by reporting key outcomes back to stakeholders.

Step 7: Promotion

Outlines the recommended communication tools and tactics to raise broad community awareness and understanding for the project, using owned, bought and earned mediums, and third-party mediums as appropriate.

Step 8: Plan

Includes the implementation plan, detailing a calendar of communications and engagement activities, recommended resources, timing and responsibilities.

Step 9: Proof

Outlines key performance indicators to evaluate the goals and objectives of the strategy.

Crafting a transformational vision and foundation narrative

Step 5 on positioning is where the stakeholder engagement opportunity comes to life through big picture positioning and story. In effect, this step is about positioning the decision or project in the minds of stakeholders through powerful storytelling. This creates a shared understanding of why the decision or project is needed now and how it will improve people's lives, now and into the future.

Casting the vision

A vision is an aspirational statement that answers the question *'what is the big picture impact, outcome or difference we aim to achieve through this decision or project that makes our community a better place to live, work and play?'*.

For example, your vision could articulate an impact in any of the following key areas:

- cultural outcomes
- social outcomes
- economic outcomes
- environmental outcomes.

Example:

'The new Blissville Community Centre will be a vibrant central meeting place where people of all ages and interests feel welcome and can come together in a spirit of mutual respect, connection and celebration.'

Crafting the foundation narrative

The storytelling framework I use for communicating the key message of the stakeholder engagement opportunity is the classic narrative structure as outlined in the section on 'Structure'. This framework ties together the past, the present and the future, giving context to the decision, project or issue and why it matters now. It enables a leader to frame the message along a timeframe continuum that helps makes sense of events.

This three-part framework is summarised as follows:

3-Act structure	Timeline	Description
Act I (the set up)	Past	**Trigger event** that changes circumstances
Act II (confrontation)	Present	**Current challenges** to be addressed caused by the trigger event
Act III (resolution)	Future	**Goal or outcome** to be achieved through the organisation's proposed solution. Includes call to action.

As with the hero's journey storyline, the protagonist hero is the stakeholder not the organisation conducting the engagement or delivering the solution. The organisation is the guide, like 'Obi wan Kenobi' or 'Yoda' in the *Star Wars* movies. Local councils, for example, are the guides who work on behalf of stakeholders and communities, who are the real heroes in the narrative.

Below are two foundation narrative examples to show how to use this structure.

Example 1:

1. *'Council's old public hall is over 100 years old and nearing the end of its life.'* **(trigger event, past)**

2. *'The building does not comply with current building codes or accessibility standards and is costing Council and ratepayers an increasing amount of money each year to maintain.'* **(challenges to address, present)**

3. a) *'Recognising the enormous value this facility provides to the local community, Council is building a larger, more contemporary community hub for the community to enjoy for generations to come. It will be a vibrant central meeting place where people of all ages and interests feel welcome and can come together in a spirit of mutual respect, connection and celebration.'* **(goal or outcome, future)**

b) *'We're conducting a comprehensive engagement process with user groups and local residents throughout the project to ensure the facility meets the needs of key stakeholders and the wider community. We encourage everyone to get involved'* **(protagonists, call to action)**

Example 2:

1. *'The inner suburb of Blissville has grown significantly in population over the last 20 years and there is now a severe shortage of community infrastructure and green space for the number of residents living in the area.'* **(trigger event, past)**

2. *'There are few social and leisure opportunities available and this has resulted in some residents becoming socially isolated, young people becoming bored and petty crime is escalating. Many people are feeling unsafe and disconnected, and community vibrancy is diminished.'* **(challenges to address, present)**

3. a) *'Council is addressing these issues by building a new contemporary multi-use community centre with adjacent park, including a skate facility and adventure play space. The new facility will provide a range of opportunities for local residents to get more active, socialise, learn new skills and come together for local events. Over time, the facility is expected to improve local health and wellbeing outcomes and community safety and foster a strong sense of community connectedness, belonging and pride among local residents.'* **(goal or outcome, future)**

   b) *'Council will conduct a comprehensive engagement process with local residents of Blissville, including children, youth, families and older people to ensure the new facility meets the diverse needs of the community. We encourage everyone to get involved.'* **(protagonists, call to action)**

Another effective framework for crafting the foundation narrative for a stakeholder engagement process is the 5Ws and H framework; for example, answering:

- What is happening?
- When is it happening?
- Where is it happening?
- Why is it important/needed?
- Who will it affect?
- How will it happen and how can people get involved?

Using these narrative frameworks helps build stakeholder trust and connection by giving a complete story and answering their key questions.

(?) Reflection questions

- How am I closing the loop with stakeholders?
- Does the wording of the engagement question enable an unbiased response from stakeholders?
- Have I set a vision for the project?
- Does my narrative follow the three-act structure to tie together the past, present and future?
- What values will I uphold in addressing the challenges?
- Who is the hero in my story?

4

Commanding the room with impactful speeches and presentations

'They may forget what you said, but they will never forget how you made them feel.'

Maya Angelou, American memoirist, poet and civil rights activist

I've always been fascinated by the way someone's words and their physical presence from the stage can cause a visceral response in an audience. I mean a deep, uninhibited response, like hairs standing on end, tears of joy or sadness, roaring laugher, deep emotion etched on faces. This is called 'moving the room' and when it happens you know the speaker has shifted something inside the people – to think and feel something differently.

As a former speech writer and advisor for many government and political leaders, I used to aim to cause a deep visceral reaction in an audience. It was a sign the message I'd crafted had been delivered with its fullest intent and desired impact. It's also one of the reasons I wanted to build my public speaking skills so I, too, could have this kind of impact on an audience because then I'd know my message was truly landing.

Whether you're the first or last keynote speaker at a conference, presenting an idea, pitching a proposal or motivating a team, transformational communication can move you beyond delivering information only to creating moments that inspire action and leave a lasting imprint.

Some of the most famous speeches in history have left an indelible mark. For instance:

- **Nelson Mandela's 'I Am Prepared to Die' speech (Rivonia Trial, Pretoria, 20 April 1964)**

Delivered from the dock during his trial for sabotage, this epic speech outlined Mandela's antiapartheid convictions and sacrifices, ending with the iconic line: *'it is an ideal for which I am prepared to die'.*[7]

- **John F Kennedy's 'We Choose to Go to the Moon' speech (Rice University, Houston, 12 September 1962)**

Courageous, visionary and unifying, this transformational speech by the then president of the United States, John F Kennedy informed the public of his plan to land man on the moon within the decade. It contained the oft quoted line, *'We choose to go to the moon in this decade and do the other things, not because they are easy, but because they are hard...'.*[8]

10 essentials for transformational speech preparation and delivery

Impactful speeches and presentations are part craft and part art. The craft involves the technical aspects of audience analysis, writing the script, structuring the information logically, and practising the technical elements of delivery. The art aspect comes through the creative expression of the words, such as nuancing the narrative with specific words for specific emotional effects. It also comes through the creative expression of the performance in the alignment of verbal and non-verbal language.

The following list distils 10 key elements for impactful speech delivery and transformational communication. Use it as a guide to command the room with purpose, power and presence, and to move people to think, feel or behave differently.

1. Have clear intent

The speech has a clear purpose; for example, to inform, educate, empower, persuade or inspire. Be clear on the mental, emotional or behavioural shift you want to create in an audience and the gift you want them to take beyond the room.

2. Structure for impact

Use frameworks to ensure a logical flow of information, to create emotional resonance and to shape a compelling narrative. Start with the basic three-act structure and hero's journey to traverse a story arc that delivers to the audience a new insight or inspiration. Remember, the audience needs to see themselves in the speech because it speaks directly to their fears, hopes and dreams.

3. Have one central message

The speech has one clear and strong core message or central argument, well supported by logical reasoning (logos) to connect intellectually and brought to life through relatable stories (pathos) to connect emotionally. Having one core message will help avoid overloading the audience with too much information.

4. Align verbal and non-verbal language

Your body language, eye contact and energy should align with your message so there is no mismatch between what you say and how you say it. Use vocal variety, such as changes in pitch, pause and pace to emphasise key points, build tension and keep the audience engaged.

5. Have a strong opening

Rather than the usual pleasantries of introducing yourself and saying how wonderful it is to be here, blah blah, start strong with a bold statement, a story, a surprising statistic or a compelling insight that instantly captures attention.

6. Have a strong closing

As with the hero's journey story arc, the hero returns with the elixir to pass on to others, end your speech or presentation with one clear takeaway insight, memorable phrase or call to action. Often called a 'mic drop moment', this powerful closing statement should also leave your audience with the desired emotional response.

7. Speak with confidence, credibility and authority

The speaker conveys good character, credibility and authority to speak on the topic (ethos). The speaker's strong conviction to the message and ability to engage the room through deliberate use of their voice and body makes it a performance.

8. Use high quality visuals

High quality, relevant photographs, images, models, symbols and other visual elements help an audience stay engaged and understand a message far more than a laundry list of bullet points.

9. Prepare and rehearse

Preparation and rehearsal builds confidence and competence. Prepare a script and practise it enough times until you can say it conversationally without reading it, otherwise you may come across as robotic. Practise saying the words and rehearse the vocal and body language elements together so they are congruent.

10. See every speech as leadership in action

Every time you speak, it's an opportunity to build rapport, shape perception and drive momentum. Treat it as a strategic opportunity.

It is these elements in combination that contribute to the impact of a speech or presentation. That's why becoming an excellent public speaker takes times, effort and practise, and experience over time.

How to write a compelling speech

There are different approaches to writing a speech, depending on the aim and audience. For instance, the goal could be to inform, educate, persuade, empower or inspire. What follows are four key elements to consider when writing a compelling speech.

1. Purpose

As with all communication, the first step is to clarify the purpose of the speech. Typically, the purpose could be multipronged, encompassing:

- **Purpose of the occasion** – clarify why the function, event or meeting is important from the organiser's perspective so you understand their goals and expectations.
- **Purpose of the speaker** – clarify why the speech is important to you. Is it to spread your message far and wide, build a public

profile, establish professional positioning in a particular niche, for example?

- **Purpose for the audience** – clarify why the speech is important for those who will hear it.

2. Audience

Take some time to understand who will hear the speech. Consider the key demographics of the audience, such as age and gender as well as their psychographics, including their beliefs, values, interests and expectations so you can tailor your message. For instance, if the audience is a group of engineers, technical jargon and data is appropriate. If, however, your audience is a diverse group of parents attending a school presentation night, you would adjust your speech to appeal to their common interests and aspirations for their children.

3. Intention

The purpose of an impactful speech is to move an audience from one state to another. In other words, to shift how they think and feel or act.

- **Think** – what do you want people to think after hearing your speech? For instance, do you want them to consider an alternative viewpoint?
- **Feel** – what do you want people to feel after hearing your speech? For instance, do you want them to feel happy, empowered, motivated or inspired?
- **Do** - do you want people to take the next step after hearing your speech? For instance, do you want them to seek more information, fill out a form, buy a book, sign a petition, change their behaviour or some other call to action?

Articulating the outcome you want to achieve guides the stories and language you use in the speech.

4. Structure

There are a variety of speech structures, depending on the purpose, timing and audience. However, what follows is a basic framework to guide your writing process.

a. Title

A two-part title works well. The first part captures attention; the second part provides a basic idea of the theme of the speech. To give examples, below are some keynote titles of presentations from a conference I organised in 2024 for local government communication professionals:

- **Beyond Roads, Rates and Rubbish** – *Harnessing the Power of Story to Foster Trust and Redefine the Local Government Narrative*
- **Are Your Residents Finding You?** – *How AI is Transforming Council Communications*
- **Lead with Gravitas** – *Timeless Skills to Communicate with Confidence and Build Trust*
- **Lessons for Building Trust** – *Challenging Assumptions and Achieving Enduring Outcomes Through Authentic Community Engagement*

b. Opening

The opening sets the scene and can be a bold statement, a short story or series of micro-stories, or both. Most often you don't need to restate your name and title as the MC would have already introduced you and the topic, and these details will be on the screen.

- **Bold statement**

  Forget the boring, '*I'm so pleased to be here...*' or '*It's my pleasure to address you this evening...*' kind of opening statements that cause people to squirm in their seats, roll their eyes and say to themselves, '*I hope this is not going to be another one of those kinds of speeches where I'd rather be at home filing my nails*'. Start with a bang instead. For instance, you could make a bold statement of claim, ask a question, share a fascinating statistic or piece of research, recite an evocative quote or any similar statement designed to grab attention, pique curiosity and connect the audience with the speaker and topic.

- **Stories**

  After your bold statement, tell a story or two. Storytelling builds rapport, trust and connection with the audience. Stories are bridges to understanding and a way of immediately establishing the audience as the hero.

  The types of stories you tell depend on the nature of the event. For instance, if I was writing a speech for a mayor to deliver at an Anzac Day event in a local community, I might write three mini stories that cascade from global to national to local scenarios.

  For instance, the first story could talk about wars on a global context; the second story could talk about Australia's involvement in wars; and the third story could talk about people from the local community who contributed to the war effort. The idea of the cascade storytelling approach is to make the topic relatable by establishing the context through the bigger picture, then establishing relevance through proximity.

c. Central idea

The central idea is a concise statement that captures the essence of the key message to be delivered. It can be a short phrase of three words, such as '*Reputation is critical!*' or it could be a stand-alone sentence that encapsulates what your speech is about.

d. Body

The body of the speech includes the main chunks of information you want to share in support of the central idea or key message. A good framework to use for the body is the 3x3 message matrix outlined in the section on 'Structure' where you have three main chunks of information and three sub-points that back up the main point.

Content chunk 1	Content chunk 2	Content chunk 3
Main point	Main point	Main point
Sub point 1	Sub point 1	Sub point 1
Sub point 2	Sub point 2	Sub point 2
Sub point 3	Sub point 3	Sub point 3

Importantly, the subpoints of each of the three content chunks must include a balance of logos and pathos in order to stimulate thinking and evoke feelings. There needs to be smooth segues between each content chunk.

e. Conclusion

The conclusion of the speech brings everything together by touching back on the central idea, the key chunks of information and even referring to the initial stories to tie off the story arc with a satisfying close.

Depending on the nature of the event, this is where the speaker would say words about those who need to be acknowledged, thanked, celebrated or recognised in some way.

Then finish with a closing statement as bold as the opening statement, such as asking a thought-provoking question, a call to action, inspiring quote or some other statement that goes full circle back and links back to the speech title or opening statement. Whatever the statement, it needs to leave the audience on a high note and hopefully, a visceral reaction.

No matter the audience or the occasion, delivering a core message and call to action through speeches and other presentations is an act of leadership. The most impactful communicators and influential leaders speak not just to be heard, but to be felt, remembered and followed.

> **(?) Reflective questions**
>
> - Have I articulated a compelling opening statement or story that will instantly create fascination, curiosity or surprise?
> - Do the main information chunks support my central idea or core message with logical reasoning and emotional resonance?
> - Does my speech follow a proven framework?
> - Have I identified the 'elixir' (key insight or transformational message) for the audience?
> - Have I identified at least three stories in my speech to bring the message to life?

5

Engaging employees and driving transformational change

'Change is not a threat, it's an invitation.'

Seth Godin, marketing thought leader and author

Change happens with or without us; however, leaders have greater opportunity to influence the way their organisation adapts, evolves and transforms in responding to change. This is because they can shape perceptions and gain stakeholder support through the power of their words and actions.

Organisational change can take many forms. For instance, cultural change, technological change, service delivery change, to name a few. While the scope and scale of individual change projects differ, what they share and what is fundamental to their success, is stakeholder support. If there's poor buy-in from those who change impacts, the change process is either going to be a bumpy ride at minimum or struggle to even launch. A study by Gartner found only 34% of all change initiatives pursued by organisations end in clear success and around half fail completely.[9]

Chief among the reasons change initiatives fail is poor communication. Research by change management specialists Prosci shows ineffective communication between leaders and employees is a stumbling block to change because there's a lack of shared vision and this results in individuals struggling to align their work with the new change. Furthermore, Prosci cautions that effective change management communication must go beyond simply telling employees change is on the horizon - *'It's about being transparent about why it's happening, what it means for them, how it will impact their position, and more'.*[10]

Ineffective communication in change management can happen at all levels of an organisation. Even if the CEO is clear to the management team about the change, if managers and team leaders, who are relied on to convey the message, are not on board with the change or do not have a good handle about why it is needed, this will impact on how well employees across the organisation understand and receive the information.

Research by Gallup[11] shows that when employees are engaged in their work, they are more emotionally connected and committed to their work and they are more likely to show resilience under stress or change. However, as highlighted earlier, Gallup's research shows that in 2024, only 21% of employees worldwide were engaged, as measured by their level of involvement and enthusiasm for work and their workplace.

With key drivers of employee engagement being 'purpose' (doing work that feels meaningful and mission-driven), 'caring managers' and 'ongoing conversations', transformational communication clearly has an important role to play in engaging employees and driving positive change.

How transformational communication facilitates successful change

Communicating organisational change requires going deeper than simply the transactional 'what' and 'how' elements, so people can understand why moving away from the status quo is needed. Transformational communication can play a pivotal role in helping leaders successfully facilitate change management initiatives by illuminating *why* the change needs to happen and creating a vivid picture of what the evolved organisation will look, feel and be like.

Here are five ways transformational communication can empower leaders during organisational change.

1. Fosters understanding through clarity of purpose

Transformational communicators articulate *why* the change matters – not just operationally, but emotionally and strategically. They connect the change to the bigger picture, helping people see beyond the current circumstances to what's possible tomorrow.

For instance, instead of saying, '*We need to change things up to stay competitive*', a transformational communicator might say, '*We are evolving some of our processes so we can continue creating an impact for our customers, while also securing our organisation's future by remaining competitive in the marketplace*'.

2. Earn trust through transparency, empathy and authenticity

People naturally resist change for a variety of reasons. For instance, they are not comfortable with uncertainty, they fear being left out or fear their future security. Transformational communication is about communicating with honesty and compassion. These leaders acknowledge the challenges while also reassuring people that they will be supported. They reinforce shared values and how these will pave the way for a collaborative roll out. This approach helps people feel safe and reduces fear, rumour and resistance.

3. Aligns hearts, minds and hands

The 'Head, hearts and hands' (3H model) transformational learning approach put forward by Orr (1992) and expanded upon by Sipos et al. (2008) can be successfully applied to organisational change.[12] That's because it recognises the all-encompassing nature of transformative experience and the importance of integrating the cognitive domain (head), affective domain (heart) and the psychomotor domain (hands) towards the achievement of a shared goal.

The holistic approach of transformational communication seeks to align heads, hearts and hands through facts, evidence and strategy (mind), storytelling, meaning and values (heart) and outlining steps to take (hands). This integrated approach increases commitment, not just compliance, and creates momentum through action.

4. Creates buy-in and shared ownership

Transformational communication is empathetic, empowering and relationship-oriented so leaders focus on collaboration and bringing people along on the journey. They invite questions, welcome feedback and facilitate participatory processes, such as codesign and cross-functional project teams.

It signals, '*We are in this together*'.

5. It mobilises momentum

Transformational communicators use vivid vision casting, relatable storytelling and consistent messaging through multiple audience channels to keep people focused on the ultimate destination and on reaching and celebrating smaller milestones. This makes the process more enjoyable and the goal seem more achievable.

In summary, transformational communication helps leaders *implement* change and *lead* it with the support of stakeholders. It turns confusion into clarity, resistance into resolve and adversaries into advocates.

A four-step framework for communicating change

Story is the essential vehicle for communicating change. In the section on 'Storytelling' we covered the remarkable power of stories in building rapport, trust and connection between people. Our brains are hardwired to be receptive to stories because, as anthropologists have found, storytelling is a human activity that dates back thousands of years. It is the quintessential way humans learn, connect and make meaning of things.

When it comes to organisational change, many people can be resistant, preferring to remain in the comfort of the status quo. This is where a strong narrative can help soften resistance and bring people along on the journey.

Barrier-breaking CEO Ursula Burns, the first Black woman to be CEO of a Fortune 500 company (Xerox, from 2009 to 2016), emphasised the importance of leaders telling stories when she spoke at the 2021 California Conference for Women. Burns led Xerox through massive transformation (from manufacturer to service provider) and when asked what that experience taught her about how people can best manage through such times of change, she said:

> *'One of the things I learned was that stories matter, communications matter. Putting things in context matters. Slowing down and telling people the reality of what's going on and giving them hope by*

providing them with the vision and idea of what it's going to look like when we get through this is fundamental. It's foundational to having people follow you.

'When you are a leader, not everyone voted for you. But at a time of struggle, even the people who aren't massive supporters are looking to leaders to help give them some context, give them some confidence, give them some idea of what they can do to help to move the ball down the road in a positive direction.'[13]

In drawing on their decades of experience helping executives lead large-scale change initiatives, Harvard Business School Professor Frances Frei and The Leadership Consortium Executive Founder Anne Morriss identify four key steps in leveraging the power of storytelling to communicate change in a 2023 Harvard Business Review article .[14]

These four steps are:

1. Understand deeply, describe simply

Understand your story so well that you can describe it in simple terms. Any communication that uses complex language or jargon only appeals to those with experience with the topic. They advise when thinking about change ask yourself: *can I capture my vision in a page, a paragraph or a word?* This reminds me of a movie logline, a concise, one-sentence summary of a television show or film that captures the core concept and hooks the audience immediately.

2. Honour the past

This step is all about recognising and communicating that the good bits about the past will be preserved. Change isn't always a case of 'throwing the baby out with the bath water'; it's about respecting and carrying forward those elements of the past that still serve a purpose while embracing the new elements. This step alone can dramatically reduce anxiety about the future because there is a sense of some continuity with the past. Honouring the past is also about being honest and dealing with negative or painful historical events that need to be recognised and addressed.

3. Provide a clear and compelling mandate for change

This step involves sharing the leader's rationale for the change and why a new desired future is preferred. This starts with conveying the 'why' behind the 'what' and the 'how'. Being specific about the problem that needs to be solved and why the change proposed is the best solution of all potential options. It's also being clear that not solving the problem will make matters worse. The arguments must be persuasive in overriding the familiarity and comfort of the status quo.

4. Describe a rigorous and optimistic way forward

This is where communication moves from the abstract to the concrete, the big picture to the nitty gritty. This is where logical reasoning is critical, where the data must tell a story – that's the rigour part of the equation. The optimism part of the equation is conveying hope and positivity for the desired future.

Enabling a storytelling culture for greater resilience

Storytelling isn't just for times of organisational change, it is most potent when embedded and enabled across an organisation. Fostering a storytelling culture can help leaders cushion the impact of, and build emotional resilience towards, the uncertainty, disruption and fear of organisational change. Storytelling also gets managers on board and brings employees into the tent.

Enabling a storytelling culture is an interplay between storytelling mindset, storytelling empowerment and storytelling synergy.

- **Mindset** is about everyone thinking of themselves as a storyteller. This paves the way for everyone to identify story opportunities and turn information into stories.
- **Empowerment** is about enabling all people across an organisation – through training, policy and opportunity – to share their stories in different ways and formats.
- **Synergy** is about people working together in a combined approach to storytelling across an organisation.

Adopting a storyteller mindset

Adopting a storyteller mindset organisation-wide requires the leader to lead by example and role model storytelling behaviour. From basic emails through to strategic meetings and delivering presentations, story must be an integral part of the information exchange.

Many organisations, especially bureaucracies, like governments, corporates and other large organisations, are conditioned to convey bulk information rather than information translated into stories. However, information only informs. Story illuminates and inspires.

Here are some ways to start embracing the mindset of a storyteller:

- before creating your PowerPoint presentation, establish the storyline
- before strategising an advocacy campaign, establish the storyline
- before embarking on a change process, establish the storyline.

Empowering staff to be storytellers

Empowering staff to share their personal stories builds trust with stakeholders by providing a window into the people behind the brand or organisation. From the people working in corporate areas to customer-facing roles, every person has a personal story they can share.

Personal stories are very important to employees as they provide an opportunity to show pride and build self-esteem. These personal stories are not only good for their personal brand; they're also building the brand's reputation.

Synergising storytelling across the organisation

When it comes to storytelling in an organisation, the whole is greater than the sum of its parts, and especially when those parts are in sync. That's why facilitating opportunities for storytelling in all parts of an organisation can magnify the overall effect.

One of the best ways to synergise storytelling is to create story rituals, opportunities for staff to be storytellers. I once read a story about a hotel owner who empowered staff to be storytellers by building a storytelling ritual. At each shift changeover meeting, the supervisor asked the staff, '*Does anyone have a story about a great customer experience they'd like to share?*' Such stories not only build employee self-esteem, they encourage a customer service ethos.

To embed storytelling across an organisation, introduce it:

- as a key element of each staff meeting
- to corporate reports
- in all presentations.
- in staff onboarding.

When storytelling is enabled across an organisation people can become a brand ambassador. Brand ambassadorship recognises that while corporate communicators and leaders are the drivers of brand communication, everyone can contribute to championing the brand. In my experience, many staff are happy to share their story about how they're making a difference through their work if they have a supportive environment to do so.

I'm not talking about a situation where anyone can say whatever they like on any platform. I've seen firsthand how that doesn't work. When I first became a communications manager in government several decades ago, the CEO allowed every employee to speak to the media without needing approval. Suffice to say, that was a tough gig to manage.

We still need guidelines and checks and balances. But what I am advocating for is an environment that empowers people to tell their story – their individual mission, their achievements, the difference they make for those whom they serve.

Helping staff to live and leave a legacy

Not long ago I was listening to an interview with Paul Dunn, cofounder of Buy One Give One (B1G1), a not-for-profit organisation that helps businesses donate a portion of their profit to just causes worldwide. He said most people tell you they want to leave a legacy. But what if you could help people live their legacy now?

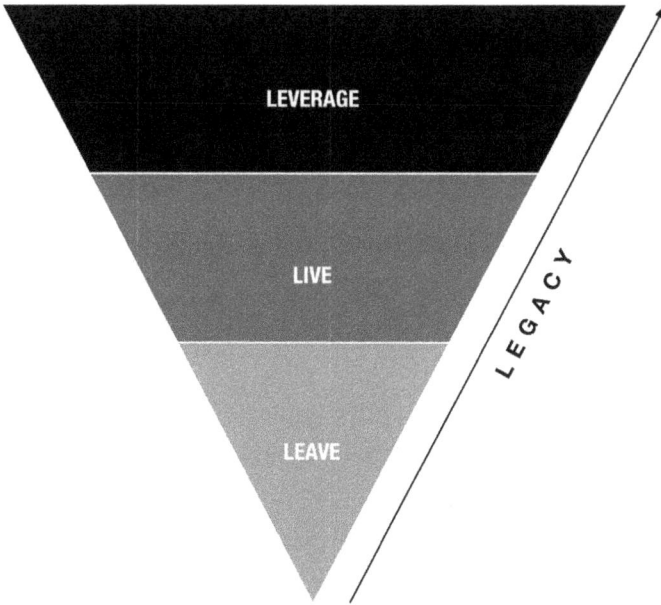

By enabling storytelling organisation-wide, leaders empower their staff to live their legacy today through sharing their work stories and the collective storytelling leverages organisational legacy exponentially.

Reflective questions

- Have I articulated the reasons *why* change is needed. Do these reasons provide a clear and compelling mandate for change?

- Have I captured the essence of the change I want to lead in an easy to explain paragraph?

- Which good parts of the organisation's past will be preserved and taken forward?

- Which painful parts of the organisation's past will be acknowledged, owned and addressed?

- What is my plan for ensuring all parts of the organisation are communicated with equally and at the same time?

- What supports and processes will be put in place to enable the airing of concerns, and the sharing of ideas and feedback?

- How could I foster a storytelling culture within our organisation?

EPILOGUE

Transformational communication is the heartbeat of people-centric leadership.

When a leader communicates with clarity of purpose and vision, strength of conviction to a bold message, authenticity and transparency, and with a warm, aligned presence that seeks true connection, every conversation is elevated beyond the transactional.

You become the leader who doesn't just deliver messages but earns trust and respect, and inspires action towards positive, lasting change.

The most influential leaders communicate with purpose, power and presence because communication isn't just a skill, it's leadership in action.

Rise as the transformational communicator you were meant to be!

ENDNOTES

PART 1

1. De Cremer, D. & Koopman, J. *Research: Using AI at Work Makes Us Lonelier and Less Healthy*, https://hbr.org/2024/06/research-using-ai-at-work-makes-us-lonelier-and-less-healthy/

2. Burley, D.L. & Long, S.D. Where do I belong? High-intensity teleworkers' experience of organizational belonging. *Human Resource Development International*, Vol 18, 2015. Issue 1, https://www.tandfonline.com/doi/full/10.1080/13678868.2014.979006

3. State of the Global Workforce, https://www.gallup.com/workplace/349484/state-of-the-global-workplace.aspx, viewed 1 August 2025

4. World Economic Forum, *The Global Risks Report 2025 20th Edition, Insight Report*. https://reports.weforum.org/docs/WEF_Global_Risks_Report_2025.pdf

5. Australian Government Electoral Integrity Taskforce, *Disinformation and Misinformation*. https://www.aec.gov.au/About_AEC/files/eiat/eiat-disinformation-factsheet.pdf

6. World Economic Forum, *The Global Risks Report 2025 20th Edition, Insight Report*. https://reports.weforum.org/docs/WEF_Global_Risks_Report_2025.pdf

7. https://www.edelman.com.au/trust/2025/trust-barometer, viewed 8 June 2025

8. https://www.nobelprize.org/prizes/literature/1953/summary/, viewed 31 July 2025

9. https://www.nationalchurchillmuseum.org/winston-churchills-speeches.html, viewed 10 June 2025

10. https://www.nationalchurchillmuseum.org/blood-toil-tears-and-sweat.html, viewed 10 June 2025

11. https://www.nationalchurchillmuseum.org/their-finest-hour.html, viewed 10 June 2025

12. https://www.nationalchurchillmuseum.org/we-shall-fight-on-the-beaches.html, viewed 10 June 2025

13. https://www.oprah.com/spirit/what-oprah-knows-for-sure-communication, viewed 12 June 2025

14. https://www.americanrhetoric.com/top100speechesall.html, viewed 12 June 2025

15. *Malala Yousafzai addresses United Nations Youth Assembly*, New York, 12 July 2023, https://www.youtube.com/watch?v=3rNhZu3ttlU, viewed 15 June 2025

16. https://www.nobelprize.org/prizes/peace/2014/yousafzai/speedread/, viewed 15 June 2025

17. https://www.britannica.com/biography/Nelson-Mandela, viewed 14 June 2025

18. https://www.britannica.com/list/nelson-mandela-quotes, viewed 14 June 2025

19. http://www.mandela.gov.za/mandela_speeches/before/640420_trial.htm, viewed 14 June 2025

20. http://www.mandela.gov.za/mandela_speeches/1994/940509_inauguration.htm, viewed 14 June 2025

21. https://journals.aiac.org.au/index.php/IJALEL/article/view/1976, viewed 14 June 2025

22. https://obamawhitehouse.archives.gov/the-press-office/2016/07/25/remarks-first-lady-democratic-national-convention, viewed 20 August 2025

23. https://www.reaganlibrary.gov/reagans/ronald-reagan/time-choosing-speech-october-27-1964

24. https://www.reaganlibrary.gov/archives/speech/farewell-address-nation, viewed 11 June 2025

25. Bell, R. Mark, 'Charismatic Leadership Case Study with Ronald Reagan as Exemplar', *Emerging Leadership Journeys Journal*, Issue 1, Vol 65, 2013. https://www.regent.edu/journal/emerging-leadership-journeys/ronald-reagan-leadership-style-charismatic-leadership/, viewed 6 June 2025.

26. https://www.reaganlibrary.gov/archives/speech/farewell-address-nation, viewed 11 June 2025

27. https://www.brainyquote.com/authors/jacinda-ardern-quotes, viewed 10 June 2025

28. https://barackobama.medium.com/conversation-at-hamilton-college-0c44228ac0bd, viewed 13 June 2025

29. https://www.president.gov.ua/en/news/mi-byemosya-za-svoye-majbutnye-svoyu-svobodu-svoyu-zemlyu-i-75989, viewed 12 June 2025

30. The Scribes Journal of Legal Writing, Vol. 13. *Justice Ruth Bader Ginsburg*, https://scribes.org/wp-content/uploads/2022/12/Scribes_vol13_09_Ruth_Bader_Ginsburg.pdf, viewed 24 June 2025

31. *Steve Jobs' 2005 Stanford Commencement Address.* https://www.youtube.com/watch?v=UF8uR6Z6KLc, viewed 31 July 2025

32. https://www.brainyquote.com/quotes/mother_teresa_142106, viewed 31 July 2025

33. https://www.oprah.com/spirit/what-oprah-knows-for-sure-communication?utm, viewed 31 July 2025

34. https://speakola.com/political/anna-bligh-flood-disaster-we-are-queenslanders-2011?utm, viewed 31 July 2025

35. https://www.brainyquote.com/quotes/winston_churchill_111314, viewed 16 June 2025

36. https://www.brainyquote.com/quotes/jacinda_ardern_954467, viewed 31 July 2025

37. https://winstonchurchill.org/the-life-of-churchill/life/man-of-words/how-churchill-prepared-for-his-speeches/, viewed 17 June 2025

PART 2

1. https://www.britannica.com/science/information-theory/Physiology, viewed 20 June 2025

2. Harvard Business Publishing. *How to Communicate for Impact.* https://www.harvardbusiness.org/insight/how-to-communicate-for-impact/

3. Kumar et al (2017), *Overcoming the effect of low self-esteem on public speaking anxiety with mindfulness-based interventions.* https://link.springer.com/article/10.1007/s40622-017-0166-4, viewed 01 August 2025

4. Centre for Creative Leadership, *The Top 20 Leadership Challenges*. https://www.ccl.org/articles/leading-effectively-articles/top-leadership-challenges/, viewed 01 August 2025

5. Hubbart, JA, *Understanding and mitigating leadership fear-based behaviors on employee and organizational success*, https://www.mdpi.com/2076-3387/14/9/225. Viewed 01 August 2025

6. https://en.wikipedia.org/wiki/Hubert_Lyautey, viewed 21 June 2025

7. https://onlinelibrary.wiley.com/doi/10.1002/9781394319831.ch12, viewed 21 June 2025

8. https://plato.stanford.edu/entries/aristotle-rhetoric/, viewed 21 June 2025

9. Kay, K & Shipman, C. *The Confidence Code*, HarperCollins, USA, 2014, p. 49

10. Cialdini, R.B. Influence, *The Psychology of Persuasion*, Collins Business, New York, 2007

11. Covey, S. *The Transformational Leadership Report*. 2007. https://iweday.web.unc.edu/wp-content/uploads/sites/9219/2015/03/TransformationalLeadershipReport.pdf, viewed 27 June 2025

12. Burns, J.M. *Leadership*, pp 43-44

13. Covey, S. *The Transformational Leadership Report*, 2007. https://iweday.web.unc.edu/wp-content/uploads/sites/9219/2015/03/TransformationalLeadershipReport.pdf

14. Westover, Jonathan H. *Transformational Communication: Strategies for Connecting and Inspiring Your Workforce*, 30 April 2024 https://www.forbes.com/councils/forbescoachescouncil/2024/04/30/transformational-communication-strategies-for-connecting-and-inspiring-your-workforce/, viewed 20 June 2025

15. Harvard Business Review, *The Business Case for Purpose*. 20 April 2016, https://hbr.org/resources/pdfs/comm/ey/19392HBRReportEY.pdf viewed 1 August 2025

16. Westover, Jonathan H. *Transformational Communication: Strategies for Connecting and Inspiring Your Workforce*. 30 April 2024. https://www.forbes.com/councils/forbescoachescouncil/2024/04/30/transformational-communication-strategies-for-connecting-and-inspiring-your-workforce/, viewed 20 June 2025., viewed 20 June 2025

17. Gallo, C. *Great Communicators Are Made, Not Born, According To Presidential Historian Doris Kearns Goodwin*, 17 Feb 2020. https://www.forbes.com/sites/carminegallo/2020/02/17/great-communicators-are-made-not-born-according-to-presidential-historian-doris-kearns-goodwin, viewed 1 August 2025

PART 3

1. Bailey, James, R & Rehman, Scheherazade, *Don't Underestimate the Power of Self-Reflection*, 5 March 2022. https://hbr.org/2022/03/dont-underestimate-the-power-of-self-reflection, viewed 12 July 2025

2. https://sdgs.un.org/goals, viewed 01 August 2025

3. Collins, J. *Good to Great: Why some companies take the leap...and others don't*, Random House, London 2001, p. 195

4. Gaines, Jeffrey, *What Is Emotional Contagion Theory (Definitions & Examples)*, 12 Feb 2021. https://positivepsychology.com/emotional-contagion/, viewed 6 July 2025

5. Kay, K & Shipman, C. *The Confidence Code,* HarperCollins, USA, 2014, p. 50

6. Cialdini, R, *Influence: The psychology of persuasion*, HarperCollins, New York, 2007

7. Sugerman, J. *Using the DISC model to improve communication effectiveness*, April 2009. https://www.researchgate.net/publication/247617924_Using_the_DiSCR_model_to_improve_communication_effectiveness, viewed 13 July 2025

8. Masen, E., Hedlund, D. & Tingle, J. *Use of DISC behavioral profiling and training: An innovative pedagogical strategy to enhance learning and future career opportunities in sport management and sport coaching higher education classrooms*, Nov 2022. https://www.researchgate.net/publication/366284379, viewed 13 July 2025

9. Wiessner, Polly. *Embers of society: Firelight talk among the Ju/'hoansi Bushmen*. https://asu.elsevierpure.com/en/publications/embers-of-society-firelight-talk-among-the-juhoansi-bushmen/, viewed 01 August 2025

10. Simon Sinek - The Golden Circle - TedTalks 2009. https://www.youtube.com/watch?v=fMOlfsR7SMQ, viewed 01 August 2025

11. https://www.aboutlearning.com/story, viewed 01 August 2025

12. Salvado, J & Vermeulen, F. 'You Should Be Able to Boil Your Strategy Down to A Single Clear Visualization', *Harvard Business Review,* July-Aug 2025. https://hbr.org/2025/07/you-should-be-able-to-boil-your-strategy-down-to-a-single-clear-visualization, viewed 06 August 2025

13. Mehrabian, A. 'Decoding of inconsistent communications', *Journal of Personality and Social Psychology.* Vol 6(1), May 1967, 109-114. https://psycnet.apa.org/journals/psp/6/1/109.pdf

14. Wakslak, C., Smith, P. & Han, A. 'Using Abstract Language Signals Power', *Journal of Personality and Social Psychology*, July 2014. 107(1):41-55. https://www.researchgate.net/publication/260714621/. viewed 23 July 2025

15. Willis, J., Todorov, A. et al. 'First impressions: making up your mind after a 100-MS Exposure to a face', *Psychological Science* https://journals.sagepub.com/doi/10.1111/j.1467-9280.2006.01750.x

16. Nair, S et al. *Do slumped and upright postures affect stress responses? A randomised trial*, National Library of Medicine. 2015 Jun;34(6):632-41 https://pubmed.ncbi.nlm.nih.gov/25222091/

Part 4

1. ABC News. *Scott Morrison says he accepts criticism for Hawaii holiday during bushfires, apologises for any upset caused.* 22 Dec 2019 https://www.abc.net.au/news/2019-12-22/prime-minister-scott-morrison-hawaii-holiday-bushfires/11821682, viewed 27 July 2025

2. ABC News. *Nixon says sorry for Black Saturday dinner*, 8 April 2010. https://www.abc.net.au/news/2010-04-08/nixon-says-sorry-for-black-saturday-dinner/2599044, viewed 27 July 2025

3. Brisbane Times. *Queensland floods 2011: A speech that rallied a devastated state.* 13 Jan 2016. https://www.brisbanetimes.com.au/national/queensland/queensland-floods-2011-a-speech-that-rallied-a-devastated-state-20160112-gm46q1.html, viewed 14 June 2025

4. De Bussy, Nigel & Paterson, Ann. 'Crisis Leadership Styles - Bligh versus Gillard: A Content Analysis of Twitter Posts on the Queensland Floods' Nov 2012. *Journal of Public Affairs.* https://www.researchgate.net/publication/264647084_Crisis_Leadership_Styles-Bligh_versus_Gillard_A_Content_Analysis_of_Twitter_Posts_on_the_Queensland_Floods, Viewed 11 June 2025

5. Joshi, P. , Wakslak, C., Huang, L. & Appel, G. 'Gender Differences in Communicative Abstraction and their Organizational Implications', *Rutgers Business Review*, Vol 6, No 2. https://rbr.business.rutgers.edu/sites/default/files/documents/rbr-060203.pdf, viewed 23 July 2025

6. VAGO, *Public Participation in Government Decision-making – Better practice guide,* Victorian Auditor-General's Office (VAGO) January 2015, p1. https://www.audit.vic.gov.au/sites/default/files/20150130-Public-Participation-BPG.pdf

7. Nelson Mandela Foundation. Nelson Mandela's *'I am prepared to die'* speech, https://www.nelsonmandela.org/news/entry/i-am-prepared-to-die, viewed 29 July 2025

8. Rice University, John F Kennedy's *'We choose to go to the moon'* speech. https://www.rice.edu/jfk-speech, viewed 29 July 2025

9. Gartner, *Organizational Change Management - Deliver on complex organizational change management initiatives.* http://gartner.com/en/human-resources/insights/organizational-change-management, viewed 29 July 2025

10. Prosci, *6 Reasons Why Change Management Fails and How to Avoid Them.* https://www.prosci.com/blog/why-change-management-fails, viewed 290725

11. Gallup, *What Is Employee Engagement, and How Do You Improve it?* https://www.gallup.com/workplace/285674/improve-employee-engagement-workplace.aspx, viewed 30 July 2025

12. Islam, Md et al. *Conceptualization of head-heart-hands model for developing an effective 21st century teacher.* 14 Oct 2022. https://pmc.ncbi.nlm.nih.gov/articles/PMC9615563., viewed 30 July 2025

13. Conference for Women. *Barrier-Breaking CEO Ursula Burns Offers Her Advice about What People Need from Leaders Now.* https://www.caconferenceforwomen.org/barrier-breaking-ceo-ursula-burns-offers-her-advice-about-what-people-need-from-leaders-now/. Viewed 18 July 2025

14. Frei, Frances & Morriss, Ann. 'Storytelling That Drives Bold Change', *Harvard Business Review*, Nov-Dec 2023. https://hbr.org/2023/11/storytelling-that-drives-bold-change, viewed 29 July 2025

ABOUT THE AUTHOR

Ros Weadman

Ros Weadman is one of Australia's foremost authorities on strategic communication. With more than four decades of experience in public relations, branding and marketing communications and multiple awards to her name, Ros has helped thousands of individuals, businesses and government organisations articulate their message, elevate their visibility and enhance their reputation.

Ros operates at the powerful intersection of purpose, principles, psychology and performance. Her approach blends strategic communication, transformational leadership theory and real-world execution to help leaders and brands get clear on who they are, what they stand for, and how to express that with authenticity and impact.

Her gift lies in distilling complexity into clarity, especially in high-stakes situations, and empowering leaders to communicate with purpose, power and presence. People don't come to Ros for fluff; they come to get equipped so they can build trust, drive change and shape the future.

Ros is a Fellow of Communication and Public Relations Australia and the author of several other books covering different aspects of strategic communication. Through her work, she's not just teaching communication techniques, she's shaping leadership identities and helping purpose-driven individuals and organisations express their vision and voice, build trust and leave a lasting legacy.